VACATION PROPERTY
SECRETS

The Insider's Guide to Investing in Vacation Properties

RODMAN SCHLEY

SB
PRESS

Dedicated to my family: Gina, Sophia, and Cecilia Schley. I love travelling throughout this world with you!

TABLE OF CONTENTS

CHAPTER 1

YOUR COMPREHENSIVE GUIDE TO SUCCESS IN THE VACATION RENTAL MARKET

f your dream is to become a part of the lucrative and enjoyable world of short-term vacation rentals, this is the guide for you. As your ally and mentor, this resource will direct you into the heart of a dynamic, profitable, and ever-evolving real estate market by offering strategies and practical insights that can propel you toward unprecedented success.

It will also be your compass, pointing you toward the path that will maximize returns in the vacation rental realm. And while there is a monetary aspect, the concepts you'll learn here will not just focus on how to make money but will include knowledge to empower you to weave your unique narrative within the vacation rental industry.

This book doesn't merely provide information—it shares a vision and strives to redefine what success looks like in the vacation property market. As you delve into these pages, you won't just be reading—you'll be embarking on a journey to unlock your potential and achieve not only success but also a meaningful, rewarding venture that aligns with your investment strategies.

Remember, every endeavor is an opportunity to be the best at what you want to be doing in life. For short-term vacation rentals, this book is the tool to help you do just that. So, absorb the knowledge and use it. Let this book guide you toward a future of fulfillment and prosperous investment strategies so you can join the ranks of those who are building their dream lives around real estate and the travel industry

VACATION RENTAL KEY OBJECTIVES

Over the last thirty-five years of my life as an entrepreneur, real estate broker, and real estate valuation expert, I have learned that one of the most important things you can do in any venture is to have a clear understanding of the fundamentals required to be successful. By focusing on the basics, I have gained years of experience and knowledge, learned invaluable investment strategies, and developed valuation methodologies to reduce risk and make wise real estate investment decisions. With my success in the industry and as the CEO of my own real estate investment company, Blue Fusion Capital, it is a privilege for me to have the opportunity to pass these fundamentals on to you.

In this book, you will get a much deeper understanding of the short-term vacation rental industry, including its growth potential, evolving trends, and the unique dynamics found in this specialized market segment and asset class. By learning the basics required to operate in this space, you will gain tremendous insight into the advantages and challenges of building your vacation home portfolio.

You will understand the process of finding the opportunities that will provide the highest rates of return. And you will learn essential topics such as property selection, market research, financial analysis, and risk assessment, as well as how to identify lucrative investment opportunities and make informed decisions when acquiring short-term vacation rental properties.

Additionally, you will gain a better understanding of the proven marketing and guest management strategies that drive bookings, increase occupancy rates, and generate positive guest experiences such as listing optimization, pricing strategies, effective communication with guests, and leveraging online platforms and digital marketing techniques.

Because one of the cornerstones for success for your vacation home rental is repeat bookings, creating a top-shelf guest experience is essential for a higher level of property performance. To understand how to take advantage of this, we will explore techniques used to enhance the guest experience and boost property performance like property staging, interior design tips, maintenance best practices, and optimizing property amenities. You will learn how to create memorable experiences that drive positive five-star reviews, repeat bookings, and guest referrals.

No business can successfully optimize returns without proper financial management. This book will provide guidance on effective financial management techniques, covering topics such as budgeting, cash flow management, expense tracking, tax planning, and evaluating return on investment (ROI). You will learn how to maximize profitability and make data-driven decisions to optimize your returns. And you will learn how to eliminate emotions from your buying and operations and how to start thinking like an investor to understand what your capitalization rates and IRR mean to the returns on your investment.

As with most every industry, the vacation home market continues to evolve at a rapid pace, so you must learn to adapt to industry changes and future trends to continue to grow. As we explore emerging trends, technological advancements, and industry shifts that could impact the short-term vacation rental market, you will gain insights into how to adapt your strategies, stay ahead of the competition, and position yourself for long-term success. You will also be equipped to handle the evolving legal and regulatory aspects as this book delves into local regulations, permits, licensing requirements, tax obligations, and insurance considerations to help you navigate the legal aspects to ensure compliance and avoid potential pitfalls.

Whether you are just starting out or seeking to optimize your existing rental business, this book will serve as a valuable blueprint, equipping you with the skills and confidence needed to achieve your financial goals and create memorable guest experiences. It will empower you with the knowledge, tools, and strategies necessary to thrive in the dynamic world of short-term vacation rentals.

BENEFITS OF INVESTING IN VACATION HOMES

Over my investment journey, I have done business in many different asset classes, but I have found that the short-term rental market is where I have gained some of the best returns. I have been able to diversify my investment portfolio and generate income which has contributed to my success.

It has also allowed me the opportunity to build a lifestyle around the ability to travel the world—something that is well-aligned with the life I want to be living. That may appeal to you, too.

The following are additional key benefits of investing in vacation homes.

Rental Income Potential

Vacation homes can become substantial revenue generators. Depending on their location and demand, these homes can be rented out to vacation-goers during peak seasons or throughout the year, offsetting property expenses, mortgage payments, and even churning a profit.

Appreciation Prospects

Sited in coveted destinations, vacation homes often hold the promise of property appreciation over time. As vacation property demand escalates, so can nightly rental rates and property values, allowing savvy investors to build equity and, eventually, sell the property for a profit.

Personal Enjoyment

Here's a perk not found in every investment—personal use! A vacation property can be a retreat for you and your loved ones to create priceless memories. It gives you the freedom to visit at your leisure and customize the property according to your tastes.

Tax Benefits

Investments in vacation homes may come with tax advantages. Mortgage interest, property taxes, insurance, maintenance costs, and depreciation might be deductible against rental income. It's vital to seek professional tax advice to understand the full scope of the specific benefits relevant to your circumstances.

Portfolio Diversification

Adding a vacation home to your investment portfolio provides a layer of diversification. Real estate has historically shown a low correlation with other asset classes such as stocks and bonds, providing stability and potential risk mitigation during market fluctuations.

Online Platforms

The surge in programs like Airbnb and VRBO makes vacation homes an ideal candidate for short-term rentals, often generating higher rental income than long-term rentals, particularly in high-demand vacation spots.

Retirement Prospects

Consider your vacation property a potential nest for retirement. As you approach your golden years, your vacation home can transform into your primary residence or be downsized to suit your needs, thus providing a comfortable living in a desirable location while reducing housing expenses.

Legacy and Inheritance

A vacation home is not merely a tangible asset; it's a vessel for your family legacy and a heritage for future generations that can create an immeasurable value for your loved ones.

Venturing into vacation home investments, while lucrative, demands careful consideration of costs, management responsibilities, market dynamics, and potential risks. Undertake exhaustive research, evaluate the financial feasibility, and seek professional guidance to make calculated investment decisions that resonate with your financial objectives and risk tolerance. Remember, successful investment is all about making wise, informed decisions that align with your goals.

AS YOU GO THROUGH THIS BOOK

This book has been designed to be a resource you can continually refer to on your vacation home investment journey. It will examine all the various steps of the buying process and give you the knowledge to make educated investment decisions to reduce your learning curve and the risks associated with a purchase of this magnitude. Vacation homes are not small investments, and your due diligence throughout the process should match the size of your investment.

If you are looking for additional tools or resources to utilize along your investment path, you can visit my personal website at gorodman.com or our short-term vacation rental website at vacationpropertysecrets.com. Both sites contain information and resources that can assist you on your vacation home investment journey.

Enjoy the book, and connect with me on social media to let me know how your investment process is evolving. I love hearing a good success story! The best place to find me is on Instagram and Facebook @gorodman. You can also find informational videos on our YouTube page at youtube.com/rodmanschley.

CHAPTER 2

UNDERSTANDING VACATION HOME INVESTMENTS

Not every home is created equally, but the great news about investing in vacation homes is that you have an opportunity to create an investment strategy around a travel lifestyle. Throughout my years as an investor, I have always looked for investment opportunities that fit the life I wanted to be living, which is close to the beach where I can settle down in a beach chair and listen to the waves while reading a book, or maybe use my sub-par surfing skills to catch a few waves.

Maybe the beach is simply not your thing, and you would rather spend your time on the golf course. Well, you are not alone. It is estimated that there are over twenty-five million golfers in the United States alone that would potentially be interested in renting your golf property when you are not occupying the space.

Whatever you enjoy doing with your leisure time, chances are good that there is a community of people who enjoy doing the same.

TYPES OF VACATION PROPERTIES

While there are many lifestyle and home options to choose from, we will cover just a few of the more common types of vacation properties.

Beach Houses

Beach houses can range from small cottages to luxurious waterfront estates and are located near coastal areas, offering easy access to beaches, water sports, and ocean views. These homes often feature large decks or patios, open layouts for views, and durable construction materials to withstand the elements.

Mountain Cabins

Mountain cabins are typically situated in scenic hilly or mountainous areas secluded from urban settings. Thanks to their cozy and tranquil setting, people come here to enjoy nature, peace, and quiet.

Features commonly found in mountain cabins include fireplaces, large windows for viewing the surrounding landscape, and outdoor amenities like decks or patios. Nearby, you can often find hiking trails, ski resorts, or other outdoor recreational activities.

Lakefront Homes

Situated directly on or near the shoreline of a lake, lakefront homes can range from simple cottages to expansive luxury residences and are designed to maximize views of the water. They provide direct access to the lake for activities such as boating, fishing, swimming, and enjoying scenic views and typically include features such as large decks, docks, or boat storage facilities.

Ski Chalets

A ski chalet is a type of residential property typically located in or near ski resorts or mountainous areas known for winter sports. They range from modest cabins to luxurious villas, and their architecture often reflects the alpine or mountain setting, featuring sturdy construction, steeply pitched roofs to handle heavy snowfall, and cozy interior design elements such as fireplaces or wood paneling.

These properties are designed with winter activities in mind, often providing easy access to ski slopes and other outdoor recreational opportunities. Many ski chalets also offer amenities like ski storage areas, hot tubs, and panoramic views of the surrounding landscape. They can be used as vacation homes, rental properties, or even year-round residences.

Condominiums

Condo units are located within condominium buildings or complexes and offer similar amenities to those found in hotels, such as furnished rooms, kitchens, and sometimes services like housekeeping or a concierge. They often come with shared amenities such as pools, gyms, and recreational facilities. Condos can be found in various settings, including beachfront areas, cities, or resort complexes, and can be a more affordable option than other vacation rentals.

Golf Course Properties

If you enjoy golfing, you might consider a vacation home located within or near a golf course. These properties can range from single-family homes and townhouses to condos and luxury estates, depending on the development.

Their primary allure is the lifestyle they offer—immediate access to golf, expansive green views, a peaceful environment, and often additional community amenities like clubhouses, pools, and fitness centers. They appeal to golf enthusiasts, individuals seeking a serene setting, and those looking for real estate in planned communities with added amenities.

Countryside Retreats

A countryside retreat is a property located in rural or semi-rural areas, away from the hustle and high energy of city life. These properties typically offer tranquil surroundings, open spaces, and a connection to nature.

Countryside retreats can vary widely in style and amenities, ranging from simple cottages and farmhouses to luxury villas and estates. They often provide opportunities for outdoor activities such as hiking, farming, horseback riding, or simply enjoying the serene landscapes.

Urban Condos

Vacation properties in popular metropolitan areas offer the vibrant atmosphere and convenience of city living, often situated close to amenities such as shops, restaurants, public transportation, and cultural attractions. They are typically part of a larger building or complex where owners share common areas like gyms, swimming pools, and sometimes even concierge services.

Luxury Estates/Villas

A luxury estate or villa is an upscale, high-end property that typically offers extensive living space and is situated on a sizable piece of land. These properties are often characterized by their exquisite architecture, high-quality finishes, and premium amenities.

Luxury estates or villas can feature multiple bedrooms and bathrooms, gourmet kitchens, home theaters, game rooms, and wine cellars, and often include outdoor features like large terraces, swimming pools, landscaped gardens, and sometimes even private access to natural features such as lakes, forests, or beaches. They are designed for comfort and privacy, and they often cater to affluent vacationers who value exclusivity and luxury living.

Remember that each type of vacation property has its own advantages, considerations, and potential return on investment. It is essential to thoroughly research the location, local regulations, market conditions, and potential rental income if you plan to rent out the property.

MARKET TRENDS AND OPPORTUNITIES

The real estate market is cyclical and always fluctuating and evolving, which allows for significant opportunities to present themselves. As an investor, it is important to always understand the current market conditions, and look at historical market conditions when making purchasing decisions. Nobody has a crystal ball to predict the future, but we can make the most informed decisions possible by having our finger on the pulse of what the market is currently doing and understanding where it is in its economic cycle.

Because the market is cyclical, having knowledge of the past provides tremendous insights into what the future could bring. For example, when the bank crisis of 2008 hit, residential real estate took a tremendous hit. People could not obtain financing, and housing prices crashed. Savvy investors took advantage of this cycle and started buying at bargain basement prices. When the market eventually started to recover, we saw incredible price appreciation through 2022 which provided tremendous opportunities for investors to make a great profit when selling their properties.

When buying short-term vacation rentals, there are multiple drivers to consider. The demand for vacation homes is driven by factors such as increasing disposable incomes, changing lifestyles, and a desire for personal getaways. Let's look at a few factors that have affected the market.

The COVID-19 Pandemic

The COVID-19 pandemic contributed to the popularity of vacation homes as people sought safe and secluded spaces for leisure and remote work. During the pandemic, adults were largely working remotely, and children were no longer constrained to physically attending their schools but instead performed their studies and classes online.

Because of this unique situation, families could relocate anywhere for any period of time, do their work and school from the vacation destination of their choice, then enjoy their vacation. The demand for short-term rentals sky-rocketed during the COVID pandemic for this very reason.

Remote Workforce

Post-pandemic, employees still often work remotely instead of returning to their offices. This has allowed individuals and families more flexibility in choosing their primary residence and vacation home locations. Many people want vacation properties that can double as remote workspaces so they can enjoy a better work-life balance and have the ability to enjoy leisure time in desirable locations.

I recently looked at a potential investment property in Nosara, Costa Rica where the sellers, who were computer programmers from San Francisco, spent their mornings surfing, followed by a day of work, then tennis in the evenings. Working remotely allowed them to live their dream lifestyle every single day.

Traditional Versus Non-Traditional Destinations

Because the way people vacation and the places they visit continue to evolve and change, the idea of what is a popular vacation destination has expanded. While traditional vacation destinations such as coastal areas, mountains, and lakefront properties continue to be sought after, emerging markets and off-the-beaten-path locations are also gaining attention as people seek unique and less crowded vacation experiences.

Municipality Restrictions

To manage the impacts of short-term vacation rentals on local communities, municipalities around the globe have been enacting a wide variety of regulations. In some cities, property owners are required to secure specific licenses or permits to legally rent their properties for short durations. Zoning rules that limit short-term rentals in certain districts have also been put in place in many areas.

Additionally, restrictions on the number of rental days per year and occupancy limits are commonplace. Homeowner Associations (HOAs) can also add another layer of regulations on property owners, including potential outright bans on short-term rentals. Furthermore, property owners may be required to meet certain safety requirements and hold specific insurance coverages.

There is also a lot of new regulation policy that revolves around taxation, with many municipalities demanding the collection and remittance of transient occupancy taxes, similar to hotel taxes. Property owners must be aware that these regulations are frequently subject to change and can greatly vary by location. Diligent research and possibly legal advice are vital to ensure compliance with current municipal restrictions.

Ease of Renting

Vacation properties have a higher potential to generate rental income than a regular property. You can use the property at your leisure, then offer it to vacationers when you're not using it via platforms like Airbnb and VRBO, which have made it easier than ever to find renters. Savvy marketers have also increased visibility opportunities by establishing a web presence and using SEO techniques to maximize their occupancy rates.

Property Value Appreciation

When buying any property, the potential exists for value appreciation (especially if you buy property in a market like 2008!). And vacation homes located in popular and growing markets have the potential for long-term appreciation. Consider areas with strong economic growth, development plans, or improvements in infrastructure that can positively impact property values over time.

Tax Considerations

It's important to understand the tax implications associated with owning a vacation home. Tax laws and regulations can vary; however, there are advantageous tax laws in place for vacation home investors. Understanding and utilizing these laws should be a part of your wealth-building and investment strategies. Many investors do not take the time to learn about these opportunities, but I would encourage you to consult with a tax professional to understand the specific tax implications of owning a vacation property in your desired location.

Lifestyle Benefits

Besides potential financial gains, vacation homes offer personal enjoyment, relaxation, and the opportunity to create lasting memories with family and friends. When evaluating the opportunities of owning a vacation property, consider the lifestyle benefits and personal satisfaction that come with owning a vacation home.

Personally, when I am looking at investment opportunities, I always look deep at the investment fundamentals, but I also concentrate on areas I like to work in and enjoy. And for my private equity fund, we have a target list of locations we feel will check both the investment fundamentals and lifestyle benefits boxes.

PROS AND CONS OF VACATION HOME INVESTMENTS

Like any investment opportunity, investing in a vacation property can have advantages and disadvantages, with different levels of risk on various investment vehicles. Consider these pros and cons when evaluating a vacation home investment:

Pros:

A vacation property can generate rental income when you're not using it. Renting out the property to vacationers can help offset the costs of ownership and potentially provide a steady stream of positive net operating income.

- Owning a vacation property provides you with a getaway destination that feels like a home away from home and the flexibility to customize the property to your preferences.

- Depending on the location and market conditions, vacation properties can appreciate in value over time. If you choose the right property in a desirable area, you may benefit from property appreciation and potentially sell it for a profit in the future. Or you could have a valuable asset that you can use as a retirement home once you hit the end of your career.

- Investing in a vacation property can diversify your investment portfolio because the real estate market has different risk and return characteristics than other asset classes like stocks or bonds have.

- There may be certain tax advantages associated with owning a vacation property like deductions for mortgage interest, property taxes, and some expenses related to property management and maintenance.

Cons:

- Purchasing and maintaining a vacation property can be expensive. Consider upfront costs such as the down payment, closing costs, and ongoing expenses such as property taxes, insurance, maintenance, and utilities. It's crucial to assess if the potential rental income and property appreciation justify the financial costs.

- Vacation properties require ongoing management and maintenance. This can involve tasks such as finding and vetting tenants, property upkeep, handling repairs, and managing bookings if you choose to rent it out. If you live far away from the property, managing these responsibilities can be more challenging.

- Real estate markets are subject to fluctuations and economic cycles. Property values may rise or fall depending on various factors such as the local economy, tourism trends, and supply and demand dynamics.

- Depending on the location and the seasonality of the area, you may have limited use of the vacation property. Some areas experience significant fluctuations in tourism demand throughout the year, meaning you might not be able to use the property as frequently or generate consistent rental income during certain periods.

- Vacation rental income can be unpredictable. There may be periods of high demand and occupancy, but also times when the property remains vacant. It's essential to consider the potential income variability and have contingency plans in place to cover expenses during low-demand periods.

- Owning a vacation property can create emotional attachments and commitments to a specific location which may limit your flexibility to explore other destinations or invest in different opportunities. Assess whether you're ready for the long-term commitment and potential limitations that come with owning a vacation property.

These pros and cons are general considerations. The specific circumstances of each individual and property can vary. It's recommended to conduct thorough research and evaluate your financial goals and risk tolerance before making a decision to invest in a vacation property.

If you do not want to purchase a property in this asset class due to the above cons, you still have an opportunity to invest in a private equity fund like the Blue Fusion Equity Fund at bluefusioncapital.com that has a portfolio of short-term vacation rental properties (I know, a shameless plug for my private equity fund!). This type of fund allows you to invest in vacation rental properties without the work required to manage and maintain this type of investment.

ASSESSING YOUR INVESTMENT GOALS AND RISK TOLERANCE

Assessing your risk tolerance when buying a vacation home is an important step in making a well-informed decision. Consider these factors when evaluating your risk tolerance in this context.

Financial Stability

Review your overall financial situation, including your income, savings, and any existing debts or financial obligations to assess whether you have sufficient funds to comfortably afford a vacation home without jeopardizing your long-term financial goals. I am a firm believer in strong financial planning and making certain that you take into account all the potential financial ramifications of this type of investment. Take the time to do the due diligence that will help you to reduce risk and lead you down the path to success.

Affordability and Cash Flow

Evaluate the ongoing costs associated with owning a vacation home, such as mortgage payments, property taxes, insurance, maintenance, and management fees. Determine if you can comfortably cover these expenses without straining your budget. When making an investment of this magnitude, it is important not to proceed before you're ready. However, with effective planning and a deep understanding of the financial requirements behind your investment, you should be able to make a wise investment decision based on your financial position.

Market Conditions

Research the real estate market in the area you intend to buy a vacation home. Analyze historical price trends, market stability, and the potential for property appreciation or depreciation. Keep in mind that real estate markets can be subject to fluctuations, which may affect your investment. Do the research and reduce the potential risks.

Rental Income Potential

If you plan to rent out your vacation home when you're not using it, assess the rental demand and potential rental income in the area. Consider the seasonality of the location and any restrictions or regulations on short-term rentals.

Diversification

Evaluate your overall investment portfolio and assess whether adding a vacation home would provide diversification or concentrate your risk in a single asset class or location. Diversification can help mitigate risk by spreading your investments across different assets.

Time Commitment and Lifestyle

Consider the amount of time and effort you're willing to invest in managing the vacation home. Owning a property requires maintenance, repairs, and potentially dealing with rental logistics or hiring property management services. Assess whether you have the time, interest, or resources to handle these responsibilities.

Emotional Considerations

Emotional factors can influence your risk tolerance and long-term commitment to the property, so it's important to determine your emotional attachment to the vacation home. Are you purchasing it solely as an investment, or do you have strong personal ties to the location?

It's important to note that risk tolerance is a personal assessment, and what may be acceptable to one person may not be the same for another. When it comes to investing in a vacation home, you should always buy based on investment fundamentals and not emotion. Take the time to do the research, then get a better grasp on your risk tolerance when developing your investment strategy.

CHAPTER 3

PLANNING AND BUDGETING

Determining a budget when buying a vacation home is crucial for multiple reasons. First, it helps potential buyers remain within their fiscal comfort zone and avoid financial strain. Without a pre-established budget, it's easy to fall in love with a property that is beyond one's financial capacity, leading to significant financial stress or even hardship. Purchasing a vacation home should be rooted in research and valuation fundamentals, not emotion.

Moreover, a well-defined budget aids in narrowing down options and simplifying the search process, saving valuable time. It also influences other essential aspects of property buying, such as location, size, amenities, and maintenance costs. Establishing a budget thus ensures a realistic and sustainable purchase, fostering financial health and satisfaction with the vacation home.

Creating your budget involves assessing your financial situation, understanding the costs associated with owning a property, and evaluating your long-term financial goals.

EVALUATE YOUR FINANCES

Begin by assessing your overall financial situation, including your income, savings, debts, and expenses. When considering a large investment, it is important that you don't jeopardize your personal cash flow. Be sure to determine how much you can comfortably allocate toward a vacation home without jeopardizing your financial stability or other important financial goals.

Because of all these costs that factor into home ownership, it's imperative that you thoroughly examine your income stability. Do you have a secure job with a steady income? Do you have other sources of income that could help offset the costs if you experience a job loss or other financial setback? Are you certain you can comfortably afford the vacation home without stretching your budget too thin?

If you don't have good safety funds in place, this could put your investment at risk if you were to lose your primary income stream. Always construct a contingency plan just in case life throws you a curveball.

If you are planning to rent out your vacation property when you are not using it, you should also estimate your potential gross rental income. When running these numbers, always be conservative in your estimates, and remember that there may be off-peak seasons where rental income might be lower. We will discuss this process more in-depth in a later chapter.

As with any investment, there are also tax implications to consider. Because owning a vacation home can have significant tax implications, including potential deductions for mortgage interest and property taxes, and potential rental income taxes, it is best to consult with a tax professional to understand these implications and take full advantage of any deductions.

Additionally, you need to think about the future resale value of a property—something very few people do. For example, when my company is making investment decisions in a market, we conservatively estimate what the resale value would be over a ten-year holding period. We first look at what kind of appreciation the market has experienced over the previous ten years, then we estimate where we are in the current real estate market, then we make an estimate of how much we think the property will appreciate over the next ten years. We also take into consideration buying in an area with good long-term prospects to help ensure that we can sell the property for a profit if we need or want to in the future.

And finally, if you plan on using the vacation home as a retirement home, consider how the costs will fit into your retirement budget. Many investors rent the home significantly during the initial phases of ownership, and then use it permanently once they retire—an excellent way to have someone else paying for your home so you can retire with a fully paid-off or reduced mortgage balance asset.

By carefully evaluating these factors, you can make a more informed decision about whether buying a vacation home is the right choice for your financial situation.

THE COSTS OF OWNERSHIP

For budgeting purposes, it is critical to consider the full range of costs associated with purchasing and owning a vacation home. This includes not only the purchase price but also closing costs and any expenses associated with owning and operating the property. All of these costs can quickly add up and exceed the purchase price of the home over time, so it's imperative that you factor them into your budget when considering a vacation home purchase to understand the ongoing financial commitments and overall affordability.

Down Payment

When estimating how much you have to spend on a vacation property, you must determine how much you can afford to put towards a down payment. Generally, a down payment of a vacation home is higher than that of a primary residence, as 20% or more is recommended to avoid private mortgage insurance (PMI) and qualify for favorable financing terms.

Mortgage Payments

If you're taking out a mortgage to finance your vacation home, you'll need to account for regular mortgage payments which will be largely affected by current interest rates.

Historically, the United States saw its interest rates plunge to an all-time low throughout 2022. This scenario began to shift when the Federal Reserve intervened to curb inflation by increasing interest rates. At the time of authoring this book, the rates had nearly doubled from the previous record lows.

On the upside, this transition has effectively reduced competition in the real estate market, notably reducing the prevalence of multiple contracts and bidding wars. However, the downside is an increase in the cost of owning a vacation home if you rely on financing, manifested in higher monthly payments.

Despite the rise, it's worth noting that those interest rates are considerably low compared to the historical standards—a great example of how important it is to look at the big picture since real estate is a cyclical market.

Property Taxes

Property taxes can vary widely by location and are often higher for second homes.

Home Insurance

Your vacation home will need to be insured, and if it's located in a coastal or flood-prone area, you may also need additional coverage, such as flood insurance.

Utilities

Your utilities for the house include costs for electricity, water, gas, internet, and waste management services. Even when you're not there, some utilities will still need to be paid, so be sure to know when each bill is due.

Maintenance and Repairs

Vacation homes also often have additional costs for maintenance and upkeep, especially if they're located in areas with harsh weather conditions or have older construction dates. Many people overlook the maintenance and upkeep costs associated with owning a short-term rental, but all homes require maintenance to stay in good shape. It's important to keep a reserve account in place for any unexpected capital expenditures that may arise during your ownership. We will talk more about maintaining a reserve account later in this book.

Furnishings and Appliances

Over time, you will have to replace worn-out or broken furniture and appliances. This is another cost that can be often overlooked but is important to include in your operating budget.

Property Listing Services

If you plan on listing your property on sites such as VRBO and Airbnb, make sure you have a clear understanding of what you as the owner must pay for these services versus what the renter is required to pay. Both sites have set fees that each party is responsible for.

Property Management Services

If you plan to rent out your vacation home when you're not using it, you may need to hire a property manager, especially if you live far away. Different levels of property management services are available, so be sure to select a provider that best suits your individual needs.

HOA Fees

If the property is part of a homeowner's association, you will need to pay regular HOA fees. However, as part of your fee, there are often expenditures the HOA will take care of. For example, on a mountain property, the HOA may take care of snow removal. If this is the case you may have higher HOA fees, but lower costs associated with cleaning and upkeep.

Travel Costs

Another frequently overlooked cost is that of traveling to and from your vacation home. This cost can add up, especially if it's far away or difficult to get to, so be sure to include it in your operating budget.

Cleaning and Upkeep

Cleaning and upkeep costs include regular cleaning, as well as tasks like snow removal or pool maintenance, depending on the property's features.

ASSESS AFFORDABILITY

It's surprising how many individuals neglect to thoroughly examine their financial circumstances before deciding to invest in a vacation home. But by not assessing affordability, you only set yourself up for failure. And ignoring potential challenges while focusing only on opportunities can lead to catastrophic results!

It is critical to take the time to analyze your budget and determine how much you can comfortably afford to allocate toward all the expenses associated with a vacation home. You should also consider other financial obligations and lifestyle choices to ensure the vacation home doesn't strain your overall financial health. Buying a vacation home should be a purchase you make with financial confidence and a clear understanding of the investment fundamentals that will lead you to excellent buying decisions.

Prior to searching for your vacation property, you should consult with a lender and get pre-approved for financing. This process gives you a better understanding of your borrowing capacity and provides a clearer picture of your budget. Also, having a pre-approval letter from a lender will increase your leverage when it comes to negotiating on a property because it lets the seller know you will be able to get the deal to the closing table.

Now, we've briefly touched on the potential costs linked to the property; however, if you have plans to rent out your vacation home during your absences, it would be prudent to calculate the potential rental income it could yield. This income can help balance some of the ownership-related costs, potentially influencing your budgetary decisions and possibly yielding a positive net operating income, contingent on the frequency of rentals.

That being said, I always advise prospective investors to maintain a conservative approach when estimating rental incomes, taking into account seasonal fluctuations and possible vacancies. It's more advantageous to *underestimate income* and *overestimate expenses*, then surpass both estimates, rather than setting your net operating income expectations excessively high only to underperform.

Unlike other investment vehicles like stocks, real estate is not a liquid asset—it's a long-term investment. Be sure to examine your long-term financial goals and how investing in a vacation home fits into your overall financial plan. And assess the impact of this investment on other goals such as retirement savings, education funds, or other investments.

Remember, it's essential to be both realistic and conservative when determining your cash flows and budgets. Better to err on the side of caution and ensure you have a comfortable financial cushion rather than stretching your finances too thin.

CHAPTER 4

FINANCIAL ANALYSIS

When considering a short-term vacation rental as an investment, performing a detailed financial analysis is paramount. This analysis will offer insight into the potential profitability of the property, help you make an informed decision, and help you optimize your investment strategy.

First, a financial analysis can help you understand the ongoing costs of owning and operating a vacation rental. This includes fixed expenses such as mortgage payments, property taxes, and insurance and variable expenses such as HOA fees, utilities, water and sewer, trash, internet and television, repairs and maintenance, marketing expenses, administration, and property management fees. You'll also need to account for potential periods of vacancy, as it's unlikely the property will be rented out 100% of the time. By understanding these expenses, you can determine how much you'll need to charge for rent to cover costs and generate a profit.

You will also be able to forecast the potential income you can expect to receive for your vacation home. This involves researching comparable rentals in the area to understand the going rental rates, as well as learning the demand and seasonality of rentals in the area.

By comparing your projected income to your expenses, you can then calculate the potential return on investment (ROI) and cash flow.

Conducting a financial analysis will also aid in assessing the property's prospects for value appreciation. Although rental earnings can contribute to a constant income flow, the appreciation of the property over time can yield substantial returns upon sale. Grasping the market dynamics and the elements that may impact the property's worth is a vital component of this analysis.

DEFINITIONS

Before we dive deep into performing our financial analysis, we will review industry definitions critical for clarity and developing a better understanding of the processes. Definitions like this are common knowledge in the real estate industry and used by real estate professionals, investors, and analysts. They can be found in real estate textbooks, financial publications, and on real estate or financial websites. For additional recommended resources on these concepts, see Appendix A.

Real Estate Purchase Price

The purchase price in real estate refers to the total amount that a buyer pays to acquire a property. This is usually the agreed-upon amount between the buyer and the seller, as specified in the purchase agreement. The purchase price includes the cost of the property itself but does not include additional costs such as closing costs, mortgage-related costs, or any repairs or improvements made after purchase.

Real Estate Closing Costs

Closing costs in real estate refer to the fees and expenses paid at the closing of a real estate transaction. This cost is in addition to the price of the property itself and can include a variety of charges such as loan origination fees, appraisal fees, title searches, title insurance, surveys, taxes, deed-recording fees, and credit report charges.

The amount due can vary greatly depending on the property, the type of loan, and local laws and customs. In general, home buyers can expect to pay between 2% and 5% of the purchase price, but, again, this can be more or less depending on the factors mentioned above.

Average Daily Rate (ADR)

In the context of vacation rentals or the hospitality industry, the Average Daily Rate (ADR) is a key performance metric that represents the average rental income per paid occupied room in a given time period. It is calculated by dividing the total room revenue by the number of rooms sold. It does not include rooms given away for free or at reduced rates.

ADR helps accommodation providers measure their performance and make informed pricing decisions. It's also useful for comparing the performance of different properties or the same property over time.

Occupancy Rate

The occupancy rate for short-term vacation rentals is the percentage of days a rental property is occupied by guests compared to the total number of days it is available for rent in a given period. It is calculated by dividing the number of days the property is rented by the total number of days the property is available for rent, then multiplying by 100 to convert the result to a percentage.

For instance, if you have a vacation rental property available 365 days a year, and it is rented for 150 of those days, the annual occupancy rate would be approximately 41%.

This metric is a vital indicator of the property's performance and can be used to make informed decisions about pricing, marketing, and maintenance schedules. A higher occupancy rate typically means that a property is in high demand and generating income, whereas a low occupancy rate might suggest that adjustments need to be made.

Appreciation Rate

In real estate, the appreciation rate refers to the rate at which a property increases in value over time. This can be due to a variety of factors including changes in the real estate market, economic conditions, improvements to the property, or development in the local area. The appreciation rate is usually expressed as a percentage increase over a specific period, often annually.

For example, if a property was purchased for $200,000 and five years later it is worth $250,000, it has appreciated by $50,000. The annual appreciation rate in this case would be approximately 4.5%.

The appreciation rate is a key consideration in real estate investing, as it can significantly impact the return on investment. It's important to note, however, that real estate values can also depreciate, or decrease in value, depending on market conditions and other factors.

Potential Gross Rental Income

Potential Gross Rental Income (PGRI) refers to the total amount of rent a property could generate if it were fully rented year round at market rates. It does not take into account vacancies, credit losses, or other potential income losses. PGRI is a theoretical maximum income figure and is often used as a starting point for estimating a property's potential profitability.

For example, if you have a vacation rental that could be rented for $200 per night, and it is available 365 days a year, your potential gross rental income would be $73,000 per year. This assumes that every single night could be rented out at that price, which is unlikely due to seasonal demand fluctuations, maintenance, and other factors.

This figure is critical in helping investors assess the income-generating potential of a property and can be used to compare different investment opportunities.

Adjusted Gross Rental Income

Adjusted Gross Rental Income (AGRI) is the Potential Gross Rental Income (PGRI) minus an allowance for vacancy and credit loss. This figure provides a more realistic estimate of the annual income a property could generate, accounting for the fact that it is unlikely to be fully rented at all times and that not all tenants will pay their rent in full.

For example, when doing an analysis on a vacation property investment, if the PGRI for a property is $100,000 per year, and the property is estimated to be occupied 65% of the time, the vacancy and credit loss allowance is 35%, the AGRI would be $65,000 ($100,000 x 65%)

Because AGRI provides a more accurate reflection of the likely rental income, it's important for investors to use this figure rather than PGRI when assessing a property's potential profitability.

Net Operating Income

Net Operating Income (NOI) in the context of short-term vacation rentals is the total potential rental income minus the total operating expenses. Operating expenses include costs like property management fees, maintenance, utilities, marketing, and property taxes, but do not include mortgage payments, depreciation, or income taxes.

NOI is a critical figure in real estate investment as it provides an indication of the property's potential profitability before accounting for capital costs like loan repayments. A higher NOI typically indicates a more profitable rental property, assuming capital costs are equal.

For example, if a vacation rental generates $75,000 in rental income per year and incurs $35,000 in operating expenses, the NOI would be $40,000 ($75,000—$35,000)

Net Cash Flow

Net Operating Income (NOI) minus debt service (i.e., mortgage payments) is often referred to as Cash Flow After Financing (CFAF) or Net Cash Flow (NCF). This important metric indicates the actual amount of cash the property is generating after all expenses, including debt service, are paid. It is the income that the investor can potentially put in their pocket, reinvest, or use to pay down additional debt.

It's important to note that while the terms "cash flow" and "net operating income" are sometimes used interchangeably in casual conversation, they technically refer to different things in real estate finance. NOI is the income left after operating expenses but before debt service, while NCF is what's left after all expenses, including debt service, are paid.

Capitalization Rate (Cap Rate)

The Capitalization Rate, often referred to as the Cap Rate, is a key metric used in real estate to estimate the potential return on an investment property, including short-term vacation rentals. The cap rate is calculated by dividing the Net Operating Income (NOI) by the property's current market value.

In the context of short-term vacation rentals, the NOI would be the total annual rental income (accounting for vacancies and other potential income losses) minus the operating expenses (such as maintenance, management fees, insurance, utilities, and property taxes, but not mortgage payments or income taxes).

For example, if a vacation rental property has an NOI of $20,000 per year and its market value is $250,000, the cap rate would be 8% ($20,000 / $250,000 = 0.08).

Cap Rate provides a useful way to compare different real estate investments and markets. A higher cap rate indicates a potentially higher return, but also typically involves higher risk, while a lower cap rate may suggest a lower return but often implies lower risk.

Average Annual Rate of Return

The Average Annual Rate of Return, often referred to as the average annual return, is a financial metric used to assess the profitability of an investment over a specified period of time. It represents the geometric average return per year over the given period, accounting for compounding.

In the context of short-term vacation rental investments, this metric would consider the property's net income (rental income minus operating expenses and mortgage payments) as well as any appreciation in the property's value over the period in question.

This metric allows investors to compare the performance of different properties or other types of investments over the same period. However, it's important to remember that past performance is not necessarily indicative of future returns.

Stabilized

In real estate, the term "stabilized" often refers to a property that has achieved a consistent and reliable income stream and occupancy rate. Stabilization typically signifies the end of major renovations or improvements, with the property achieving a predictable state of expenses and returns. Stabilized properties are not likely to have large amounts of vacant space and have predictable expenses. Therefore, investors often seek these types of properties for their portfolios.

BUILDING THE PROFORMA

Now that we have a good grasp on the definitions that will be used throughout our financial analysis, we can start to develop our projected operating statement (proforma) and estimate our year-one stabilized cash flow and net operating income.

To assist you in this process, I highly recommend using our FREE valuation tool calculator. This tool takes your assumptions and inputs and automatically calculates the formulas discussed in this chapter. It serves as our initial step in evaluating whether a vacation home is worth considering.

As a rule, we eliminate properties that do not meet a capitalization rate of at least 10%. However, it is important to tailor your investment criteria to align with your specific goals and fundamental investment principles.

If you would like to receive a **FREE** Excel file giving you access to our fully functional proforma operating statement template we use throughout this chapter, please visit vacationpropertysecrets.com/freevaluationtool. The template is fully automated and comes with complete instructions on how to properly use the tool.

In addition to the free valuation tool, we offer a boot camp course on how to use this tool to its full potential. The tool is free, and the boot camp course is inexpensive and will help you master these valuation methodologies.

COMPLETED PROFORMA

Before we go through each step required to properly complete your stabilized year-one operating statement, here is an example of what it will look like completed. (Note: for calculation simplicity, an interest-only loan is used in this model.)

STABILIZED YEAR 1—SHORT TERM VACATION RENTAL CASHFLOW

Assumptions				
Total Purchase Price	$750,000	100%	ADR	$525
Loan Amount	$525,000	75%	Days Available	365
Cash Amount	$225,000	30%	Occupancy Rate	65%
Interest Rate	6.50%			
Effective Gross Rental Income	**$124,556**	16.61%	% of Purchase Price	

Property Expenses				
Fixed Expenses				
Taxes	$4,000	3.21%	Historical	Annually
Insurance	$2,000	1.61%	Market	Annually
Variable Expenses				
HOA	$3,000	2.41%	Historical	Annually
Gas/Electric	$3,500	2.81%	Historical	Annually
Water Sewer	$1,200	0.96%	Historical	Annually
Trash	$0	0.00%	Historical	Annually
Internet/TV	$0	0.00%	Historical	Annually
Repair and Maintenance	$3,000	2.41%	Historical	Annually
Miscellaneous	$0	0.00%	Historical	Annually
Miscellaneous	$0	0.00%	Historical	Annually
Administration	$1,868	1.50%	Market	Annually
Property Listing Services	$3,737	3.00%	Market	Annually
Management Fee	$18,683	15.00%	Market	Annually
Total Property Expenses	**$40,989**	32.91%		
Total Net Operating Income	**$83,568**	67.09%		
Year 1: Stabilized Capitalization Rate	**11.14%**			
Less: Interest Only Loan Expenses	$34,125			
Total Net Cashflow (After Debt Service)	$49,443			
*Year 1: Stabilized Average Annual Rate of Return	**21.97%**			

* Does not Include appreciation or inflation over the holding period

As you can see above, you will need a firm understanding of the definitions provided at the beginning of this chapter. It is also important to note that this is a basic operating statement that should be used to do your initial property income analysis. It does not include appreciation or inflation over the holding period (that can be added at the end of the analysis) and also does not take into account any time required to bring the property up to stabilized occupancy.

ESTIMATING THE EFFECTIVE GROSS RENTAL INCOME

In calculating the effective gross rental income, we will be using this portion of the operating statement. (If you do not download our free spreadsheet, you will need to create your own based on the following assumptions and methodologies.)

In the free proforma we provide, the first assumptions you will input include total purchase price, loan amount, cash amount, and interest rate. These will be utilized later in the valuation.

STABILIZED YEAR 1—SHORT TERM VACATION RENTAL CASHFLOW				
Assumptions				
Total Purchase Price	$750,000	100%	ADR	$525
Loan Amount	$525,000	75%	Days Available	365
Cash Amount	$225,000	30%	Occupancy Rate	65%
Interest Rate	6.50%			
Effective Gross Rental Income	**$124,556**	16.61%	% of Purchase Price	

Purchase Price

Estimating the purchase price is typically straightforward. At this stage of your assessment, it is likely that you haven't made an initial offer on the property you're considering. When I spot a property that piques my interest, I tend to use its listed price for my assumptions. While you may end up negotiating a more favorable price, this method provides a suitable conservative figure for your analysis.

Note that this total cost does not account for any closing costs or potential improvements the property might need. If you want to evaluate how these additional expenses affect your return on investment, incorporate them into the listing price in your assumptions.

In the case of this example, we are estimating the total purchase price at **$750,000**.

Loan/Cash Amounts

This estimate is simply how much you intend to borrow and how much you will pay in cash. These assumptions will be taken into consideration later in the analysis once you have estimated your total net cash flow (after debt service) and estimate your stabilized average annual rate of return. If you are paying cash and do not want to leverage the property, you can simply add $0 to the loan amount, and put 100% of the purchase price in the cash amount.

In the case of this example, we are estimating the total loan amount at **$525,000**, and the cash amount at **$225,000**.

Interest Rate

Interest rates tend to fluctuate. To simplify the process, you can use current market interest rates to estimate how much your loan will cost annually. This assumption will be taken into consideration when calculating the interest-only loan expense later in the analysis.

In the case of this example, we are estimating the interest rate at **6.5%**.

When projecting what our effective gross rental income will be, a certain set of assumptions must be determined. The assumptions that need to be estimated include average daily rate, days available, and occupation rate.

Average Daily Rate (ADR)

Determining the Average Daily Rate (ADR) for vacation home investments can be a nuanced process as it requires careful consideration of numerous factors, both tangible and intangible.

The first and perhaps most straightforward method in determining the ADR is to perform a Comparative Market Analysis (CMA). This involves comparing your property to similar ones in the area, focusing on features such as size, amenities, and proximity to local attractions. Various online platforms like Airbnb and VRBO can provide a wealth of data about average rates for comparable properties. You can also utilize specialized tools like AirDNA and Mashvisor that provide in-depth market analysis for vacation rentals.

We use AirDNA and their rentalizer tool when we are determining our ADR. It has been proven to be both accurate and reliable. However, if you do not want to use a paid tool like AirDNA, you can also look on VRBO at properties in the neighborhood you are considering. If you do not put in a date range, VRBO will list the ADR for comparable properties you can use in your comparison. Remember, you do not want the rental rate for a specific date or date range. The ADR is the Average Daily rate based on a 365-day period.

In the case of this example, we are estimating the ADR at **$525**.

Days Available

The days available is the number of days that you want to make the vacation home available for rent. If you plan on blocking 100 days off on the calendar for your personal use, put 265 days in for this assumption. If you plan on having the property available for rent for 365 days, and only using the property when it is not rented, put 365 days in for this assumption.

In the case of this example, we are estimating the days available at **365 days**.

Occupancy Rate

In order to proceed with this section of the analysis, we need to make one final assumption regarding the projected occupancy rate. To simplify the process of projecting the occupancy rate, we rely on AirDNA data, which leverages a decade's worth of historical information from both Airbnb and VRBO to estimate the potential occupancy rate for a property. This estimation is an integral part of AirDNA's rentalizer tool, facilitating the projection of occupancy rates effortlessly.

However, if you prefer not to use a paid tool like this, there are alternative approaches you can consider. One option is to reach out to management companies in the area and inquire about the occupancy rates they have observed for properties similar to the one you are contemplating. Alternatively, local real estate brokers can also serve as a valuable resource in providing such information. Another approach involves reviewing the rental calendars of comparable properties to gauge their level of bookings and using that data to estimate a projection. It is worth noting that the more time and effort you dedicate to estimating this projection, the greater the accuracy of your operating statement will be.

In the case of this example, we are estimating the occupancy rate at **65%**.

EFFECTIVE GROSS RENTAL INCOME

Now that we have completed our first set of assumptions, we are able to estimate the Effective Gross Rental Income for the property we are considering. The formula for this estimate is:

- **ADR x Days Available x Occupancy Rate = Effective Gross Rental Income**

Or in the case of our example:

- **$525 (ADR) x 365 (Days Available) x 65% (Occupancy Rate) = $124,556 (EGRI)**

This is the total amount of money we are projecting to make before we pay the expenses associated with the vacation home that we are purchasing.

ESTIMATING THE OPERATING EXPENSES

Projecting operating expenses for an investment property is crucial in understanding its potential profitability and feasibility. The process involves several steps that require both research and a solid understanding of real estate investment dynamics.

When it comes to operating expenses, you must first identify all the potential operating expenses that will be associated with the property you are taking into consideration.

For short-term vacation home properties, these expenses typically consist of:

- Property Taxes
- Insurance
- HOA
- Gas and Electric
- Trash
- Internet and Television
- Repairs and Maintenance
- Administration
- Property Listing Services
- Management Fees

It is crucial to ensure all operating expenses are included in your cash flow projections; however, the categorization of expenses can be customized according to your preferences. As a general practice, we typically allocate items such as cleaning, pool upkeep, and lawn care to the repairs and maintenance category.

Certain costs, like property taxes and insurance, can usually be estimated with a high degree of accuracy. On the other hand, repair and maintenance costs are more challenging to predict accurately and may require assumptions based on historical data and industry standards.

The next step involves gathering data. Start by obtaining the property's historical operating expenses if they are available. This information may not always be readily accessible though, especially for residential properties, and can depend on the sophistication of the seller.

If you are unable to find this data, consulting with local property managers or other real estate professionals can provide valuable insights into typical expenses in the area. Additionally, remember to account for inflation rates in your calculations to accurately project future expenses. To demonstrate accurate expense projections, we will conduct a case study at the end of this chapter.

When it comes to repair and maintenance costs, it is generally advisable to allocate a percentage of the property's value each year for these expenses. The exact percentage may vary, but a common recommendation is 1-2% of the property's value per year, depending on the expenses included in this estimate. This approach ensures you are prepared for any unforeseen costs that may arise.

Another essential consideration is building a reserve account to address unexpected capital improvement items during your ownership, such as a malfunctioning furnace or dishwasher. Although these expenses are not factored into your cash flow projections because they are considered capital improvements, it is prudent to set aside reserves for unforeseen issues.

Even with careful planning and research, unexpected expenses can occur. A contingency allowance serves as a financial buffer to absorb these surprises without significantly impacting your investment's profitability. A common practice is to allocate around 6% to 10% of your total estimated operating expenses for contingencies.

In terms of best practices, our private equity fund typically requests three years of historical operating information for the property. Historical operating expenses provide the most reliable resource for making projections. By examining historical expenses, you can observe trends for each expense over a three year period.

For example, have insurance costs been increasing, and at what rate? What about gas and electric expenses? Understanding past trends enables better estimation of future outcomes. While obtaining three years of data may not always be possible, it is advisable to inquire about it.

If historical data is unavailable, the next step involves gathering market data to support your projections. To do so, you may have to do a bit of research to gather data on each kind of expense. Here are a few suggestions that may help collect that information.

Property Taxes

Real estate taxes represent a significant expense for vacation home property owners. Therefore, conducting thorough research on real estate taxes is essential for understanding the overall costs associated with owning a vacation home.

In cases where historical data is unavailable, you can visit the website of the local municipality or county where the property is situated. Look for the tax assessor's office or department, as they typically provide tax rate information either on their website or upon request. It may also be possible to find the property's current assessed value and previous tax bills, which can provide valuable insights into what to anticipate.

Keep in mind that property taxes can vary significantly depending on the property's location and assessed value and are often higher compared to primary residences, as many municipalities impose higher rates on non-residential properties. And when examining a previous tax bill, consider the potential for tax increases. Taxes are linked to the assessed values of the real estate, and if you are purchasing a vacation home in a market experiencing property value appreciation, there is a strong likelihood that you may need to adjust your tax projections accordingly.

Insurance

When researching insurance costs for a vacation home, contact insurance companies that offer coverage in the area where your home is located, making sure to obtain quotes from multiple insurers to compare rates and coverage options. When requesting quotes, provide detailed information about the property, including its size, age, construction type, and any safety features it possesses, such as alarm systems or fire sprinklers. Additionally, take into account the location's vulnerability to natural disasters such as floods, hurricanes, or wildfires, as these factors can have a significant impact on insurance costs.

Another important factor to consider is whether you plan to rent out the home when you're not using it, as this can also affect your insurance requirements and costs. Because it is essential to thoroughly understand the coverage and exclusions of each policy to ensure that you have adequate protection for your vacation home, engaging the services of an insurance broker who has knowledge of the local market can be highly beneficial during this process.

Homeowners Association (HOA) Fees

HOA fees are typically disclosed in the real estate listing agreement. Once you have confirmed the vacation home you are interested in is part of an HOA, you can directly contact the HOA or ask your real estate agent to gather the necessary details.

Request information about the current HOA fee, what it covers, the frequency of payments, and the historical rate of increases, and determine if there are any potential changes or upcoming capital improvements that could impact those costs. Some HOA fees include amenities such as landscaping, trash removal, snow removal, or access to community facilities like pools or gyms.

If certain items included in the HOA fees are already accounted for in your proforma, ensure that your cash flow projections do not duplicate the expense. For example, if trash removal is covered by the HOA fee, you should enter $0 for trash in your operating statement.

Additionally, inquire about any planned special assessments, which are costs beyond the regular HOA fee that homeowners may need to pay. These special assessments are typically for larger, infrequent expenses like roof replacements or major repairs and are a critical consideration. For example, HOAs often require work such as exterior painting or roof replacements and divide the costs for such projects among the owners.

And finally, request a copy of the HOA's financial statements to ensure its financial health. All of these steps will give you a crucial and comprehensive understanding of the financial impact of HOA costs before making a decision to purchase a vacation home.

Gas and Electric

When researching potential gas and electric costs for a vacation home, the first step is to identify the utility providers serving the area. In many cases, owners have access to historical data for this expense category; however, if historical data is not available, you can contact utility companies directly to gather the necessary information.

Understanding the seasonal variation in utility costs is significant for a vacation home. Factors such as the home's size, the age and efficiency of its heating and cooling systems, and the quality of insulation should be taken into account when considering these costs. Inflation should also be accounted for, as energy prices typically rise each year. Neglecting to account for inflation can have a negative impact on your cash flow projection.

You also must consider any differences in usage. For instance, if you plan to rent out the property when you're not using it, you may encounter higher utility costs. Additionally, local weather patterns and energy costs in the region can significantly influence the overall utility expenses.

Water and Sewer

Researching potential water and sewer costs for a vacation home involves understanding both the usage and rate structure in the property's area. Keep in mind that costs can fluctuate seasonally, especially for a vacation home, and if the home has been vacant for periods of time, the costs could potentially be lower than expected when the home is occupied.

To gather information, contact the local water and sewer companies to understand the rate structure, which may include base fees plus usage charges. Rates can vary greatly depending on the municipality. If the home has a septic system instead of sewer service, consider the potential costs of maintenance and eventual replacement. Additionally, if you plan to rent the vacation home, anticipate higher usage and costs.

Trash

When researching potential trash removal costs for a vacation home, start by finding out which company provides waste removal services in the area. This service may be managed by the municipality or a private waste management company. Contact the provider to inquire about their pricing structure, which can depend on factors such as pick-up frequency, container size, and inclusion of recycling services.

If the current homeowner or a neighbor uses a similar service, they may provide a cost estimate, but keep in mind that if you plan to rent out the vacation home, the amount of waste generated may increase, necessitating more frequent pick-ups. Additionally, find out if there are additional costs for disposing of larger items, as this can be relevant if you're planning renovations or updates to the property.

Internet and Television

Identify available service providers in the property's location, then visit the providers' websites or contact them directly to understand their pricing structures. Consider the level of service needed, such as reliable high-speed internet for attracting guests who require remote work capabilities. For television, weigh the option of streaming services versus traditional cable, depending on guest preferences. In some areas, the choices for internet and television may be limited, especially in remote vacation locales.

Repairs and Maintenance

Researching potential repair and maintenance costs for a vacation home can be a complex task as these costs can vary widely depending on the property's age, condition, and location. But there is nothing worse than purchasing a vacation home only to discover there are significant repairs and maintenance items that need to be accommodated, so it pays to do the research on the front end.

Begin by hiring a professional home inspector to examine the property thoroughly. They can identify any existing issues and provide an estimate of the cost to fix them. This inspection can also help you understand the lifespan of major systems and appliances, like the roof, HVAC system, and water heater, allowing you to anticipate when these might need replacement.

Your repairs and maintenance budget should be tailored specifically based on the projected need for ongoing repairs. A property by the ocean may have higher ongoing repair needs due to the impact of the ocean mist on the dwelling, and an older property will likely have higher repair needs than a newer property.

Also, when you rent out the property, you might face higher maintenance costs due to increased wear and tear. Historical operating data is usually the best indicator to project the future repairs and maintenance costs specifically related to the property that you are considering buying. However, if this is not available, consulting with local property managers or contractors can also provide valuable insights into typical repair and maintenance costs in the area.

Administration

When researching potential administrative costs for a vacation home, take into consideration items related to bookkeeping, tax preparation, contract preparation, legal fees, and more, but exclude any costs already covered by management fees. Budget for travel costs if you don't reside near your vacation home and need occasional visits to check on the property.

As a general rule, allocate 1% to 3% of the effective gross rental income for potential expenditures.

Property Listing Services and Marketing Costs

First, identify popular rental platforms in the area, such as Airbnb, VRBO, or local real estate agencies, and check their fee structures— these services often charge a percentage of the booking amount, ranging from 3% to as high as 20%. There are a significant number of property listing platforms, so take the time to determine which platforms will provide you with the best opportunities for booking at the most competitive pricing.

Marketing costs might also include paid advertising on social media or search engines, which will depend on your target audience and the competitiveness of the market. Additionally, if you plan on creating a website for your property, there could be ongoing hosting fees, URL registration fees, and website maintenance that should be accounted for.

Property Management

Property management fees typically range from 10% to 30% of the monthly rental income. These fees typically cover services such as finding and screening tenants, handling tenant issues and emergencies, collecting rent, and managing repairs. Some companies charge a lower monthly percentage but may have additional fees for services like setup, tenant placement, or lease renewal.

Remember to ask what services are included in their basic fee and what services will incur additional charges. It's also wise to review their contract terms to understand obligations and potential penalties for early termination. Remember, while a property management company will add to your expenses, it can also save you considerable time and hassle, especially if you live far from your vacation home or if it's frequently rented out.

Miscellaneous Expenses

Depending on the specific property and location, there may be additional operating costs to consider like security systems, property taxes related to short-term rentals, licensing fees, local permits, or any required inspections.

As an example, with our Costa Rica properties, we are required to pay a luxury tax on the homes we own because they meet a higher value threshold. This tax is in addition to the typical real estate property taxes we are required to pay.

ADDING PROJECTED OPERATING EXPENSES TO THE PROFORMA

Now that we have estimated our operating expenses, we can add them into our operating statement. This section of your proforma should look something like this:

Property Expenses				
Fixed Expenses				
Taxes	$4,000	3.21%	Historical	Annually
Insurance	$2,000	1.61%	Market	Annually
Variable Expenses				
HOA	$3,000	2.41%	Historical	Annually
Gas/Electric	$3,500	2.81%	Historical	Annually
Water Sewer	$1,200	0.96%	Historical	Annually
Trash	$0	0.00%	Historical	Annually
Internet/TV	$0	0.00%	Historical	Annually
Repair and Maintenance	$3,000	2.41%	Historical	Annually
Miscellaneous	$0	0.00%	Historical	Annually
Miscellaneous	$0	0.00%	Historical	Annually
Administration	$1,868	1.50%	Market	Annually
Property Listing Services	$3,737	3.00%	Market	Annually
Management Fee	$18,683	15.00%	Market	Annually
Total Property Expenses	**$40,989**	32.91%		

When making projections, it is good to note if the estimate is based on historical or market data, and what percentage of the income the expense equates to. When we have good data, this allows us to compare our projected operating expenses with other similar properties.

For example, in the above estimate, the operating expenses were projected at **32.91%** of the effective gross rental income. If the range of expenses for the other properties we were looking at was 28% to 35%, this would indicate that our expenses are within the range of comparable properties and would support our expense estimate.

However, if the range of comparables was 25% to 30%, we would want to do some additional due diligence to see why our estimate is outside of (and in this case above) the range of comparable properties. There might be a good reason, but additional research would be warranted.

CALCULATING OUR NOI

Now that we have estimated our Effective Gross Rental Income (EGRI) and estimated our projected operating expenses, we can project the Net Operating Income (NOI) for the vacation property. Putting these elements into a proforma looks like the form on page 54.

STABILIZED YEAR 1—SHORT TERM VACATION RENTAL CASHFLOW

Assumptions				
Total Purchase Price	$750,000	100%	ADR	$525
Loan Amount	$525,000	75%	Days Available	365
Cash Amount	$225,000	30%	Occupancy Rate	65%
Interest Rate	6.50%			
Effective Gross Rental Income	**$124,556**	16.61%	% of Purchase Price	
Property Expenses				
Fixed Expenses				
Taxes	$4,000	3.21%	Historical	Annually
Insurance	$2,000	1.61%	Market	Annually
Variable Expenses				
HOA	$3,000	2.41%	Historical	Annually
Gas/Electric	$3,500	2.81%	Historical	Annually
Water Sewer	$1,200	0.96%	Historical	Annually
Trash	$0	0.00%	Historical	Annually
Internet/TV	$0	0.00%	Historical	Annually
Repair and Maintenance	$3,000	2.41%	Historical	Annually
Miscellaneous	$0	0.00%	Historical	Annually
Miscellaneous	$0	0.00%	Historical	Annually
Administration	$1,868	1.50%	Market	Annually
Property Listing Services	$3,737	3.00%	Market	Annually
Management Fee	$18,683	15.00%	Market	Annually
Total Property Expenses	**$40,989**	32.91%		

In the example above, we estimated an Effective Gross Rental Income of **$124,556** based on the projected ADR of $525, the Days Available of 365, and the projected Occupancy Rate of 65%.

The formula for this calculation is:

- **$525 ADR x 365 Days Available x 65% Occupancy Rate = $124,556 EGRI**

Next, we estimated the Total Property Expenses at **$40,988**, which was based on a mix of historical and market information. With these projections in place, we can simply deduct our Total Property Expenses from our Effective Gross Rental income to estimate our Net Operating Income.

The formula for this calculation is

- **$124,556 EGRI—$40,988 Property Expenses = $83,568 NOI**

CAPITALIZATION RATE

Now that we have a projected NOI, we can estimate the Capitalization Rate to project our potential return on our investment if we were to pay cash. The formula to estimate a capitalization rate is Net Operating Income / Purchase Price.

In this case, the NOI is estimated at $83,568, and the Purchase Price is estimated at $750,000. Therefore, the calculation of the capitalization rate based on these assumptions is

- **$83,568 NOI / $750,000 Purchase Price = 11.14% Cap Rate**

IMPACT ON RETURNS THROUGH LEVERAGING

Next, we want to do a calculation to determine if we should leverage our investment with a loan or financing vehicle. For simplicity's sake, for these calculations we will model an interest-only loan which would require the same interest cost monthly over the holding period. By going through this methodology, you can determine how an interest rate can impact your annual rate of return.

STABILIZED YEAR 1—SHORT TERM VACATION RENTAL CASHFLOW

Assumptions				
Total Purchase Price	$750,000	100%	ADR	$525
Loan Amount	$525,000	75%	Days Available	365
Cash Amount	$225,000	30%	Occupancy Rate	65%
Interest Rate	6.50%			
Effective Gross Rental Income	**$124,556**	16.61%	% of Purchase Price	
Property Expenses				
Fixed Expenses				
Taxes	$4,000	3.21%	Historical	Annually
Insurance	$2,000	1.61%	Market	Annually
Variable Expenses				
HOA	$3,000	2.41%	Historical	Annually
Gas/Electric	$3,500	2.81%	Historical	Annually
Water Sewer	$1,200	0.96%	Historical	Annually
Trash	$0	0.00%	Historical	Annually
Internet/TV	$0	0.00%	Historical	Annually
Repair and Maintenance	$3,000	2.41%	Historical	Annually
Miscellaneous	$0	0.00%	Historical	Annually
Miscellaneous	$0	0.00%	Historical	Annually
Administration	$1,868	1.50%	Market	Annually
Property Listing Services	$3,737	3.00%	Market	Annually
Management Fee	$18,683	15.00%	Market	Annually
Total Property Expenses	**$40,989**	32.91%		
Total Net Operating Income	**$83,568**	67.09%		
Year 1: Stabilized Capitalization Rate	**11.14%**			
Less: Interest Only Loan Expenses	$34,125			
Total Net Cashflow (After Debt Service)	$49,443			
*Year 1: Stabilized Average Annual Rate of Return	**21.97%**			

In this example, we are considering an interest-only loan at 6.5% and borrowing 70% of the purchase price. Therefore, our annual loan expenses are estimated at **$34,125 ($525,000 x 6.5%)**. Because it is interest only, there would be no principal deduction each month as no portion of the payment would be allocated to and deducted from the loan balance.

In order to estimate the Total Net Cash Flow (After Debt Service), we need to subtract the annual Loan Expenses from the Net Operating Income. Therefore, the Total Net Cash Flow (after debt service) is estimated at **$49,443 ($83,568 NOI—$34,125 Loan Expenses)**.

In this case, our Net Operating Income has gone down to accommodate the loan payments; however, because we are partially financing the property, the amount of money we had to pay out of pocket to purchase the property has also declined. Based on the 30% cash we have now put down on this property, our cash investment is now $225,000.

Therefore, in order to calculate the return on our investment based on leveraging the property, we must now divide the Total Net Cashflow by the Cash Investment. This will give us our Projected Annual Rate of Return. In this example, the Projected Annual Rate of Return is estimated at **($49,443 Net Cashflow / $225,000 Cash Investment) = 21.97% Annual Rate of Return**.

Based on these calculations and assumptions, the return on investment would increase significantly by using financing and leveraging the investment. As you can see in the calculations and assumptions, if the interest rate goes up, the Annual Rate of Return would go down. If the NOI goes down, so would the Capitalization Rate and the Annual Rate of Return.

Every assumption throughout this analysis has an impact on your overall projections and returns. This is why it is so important to take your time and do the due diligence necessary to accurately complete this analysis. Small mistakes can and will have an impact on your valuation methodology.

APPRECIATION, RENTAL RATE GROWTH, AND INFLATION

Before we move on to the next chapter, I do want to point out that this is the projected income stream for a single year and does not take into account inflation or appreciation. The returns previously calculated only take into consideration how you project the property will perform in year one when you have stabilized the property.

Throughout the duration of owning your vacation home, it is reasonable to anticipate fluctuations in rental rates, expenses, and the property's value. Ideally, you would hope for rental rate growth that matches or surpasses the inflation of property expenses, along with property value appreciation that enhances the returns projected in your proforma.

Once you have conducted this analysis, you can further conduct market research to ascertain the historical property value appreciation in the market where you are contemplating a purchase.

METHODS FOR ESTIMATING APPRECIATION

Projecting property value appreciation for a vacation home involves analyzing both historical data and future trends in the real estate market. However, it is important to note that real estate appreciation is never guaranteed and can be influenced by a wide range of factors.

Begin by researching historical property value trends in the specific area where your vacation home is located. Real estate websites, local government property records, and real estate agents can provide valuable data about how much properties in the area have appreciated over time. However, remember that past performance is not a guarantee of future results.

You should also consider factors that may affect future appreciation. These can include local economic trends, population growth, and infrastructure developments. For example, a new school, shopping center, or transportation hub being built nearby could potentially boost property values.

Another factor to consider is the overall condition and features of your home. Regular maintenance and updates can help the property retain its value and potentially increase it over time. Conversely, deferred maintenance and outdated features can decrease a property's value.

Also consider the demand for vacation rentals in your area, as strong rental demand can boost property values. Trends in tourism, local attractions, and even changes in travel habits can influence this.

Despite all this, it is crucial to remember that property value appreciation projections are still ultimately estimates. The real estate market can be unpredictable, and numerous factors can impact property values. Therefore, while appreciation can significantly contribute to the return on a real estate investment, it is generally not advisable to rely on it as the primary source of potential profit.

VALUATION CASE STUDY

In our first case study, we will examine a property listed for sale in Costa Rica.

FOR SALE: $900,000

BEDROOMS:	4 Bedroom	**SQUARE FEET:**	4.200 SF
BATHROOMS:	4 Bathrooms	**LOT SIZE:**	12.390 SF
SLEEPS:	10 People	**FURNISHED:**	Fully

The property is located in Costa Rica, has excellent ocean views, and is a short 5-minute walk to the beach and town. The investor was provided with the prior year's historical expense data for the property; however, the home has not historically been operated as a short-term vacation rental, so there is no historical revenue information available.

INCOME AND EXPENSE DATA

No historical rental revenue data was provided; however, the investor was provided with the prior year's expense data. The projected ADR and Occupancy were based on comparable properties in the market.

Historical operating data was provided for the previous year. Historical real estate taxes and gas/electric were inflated by 3% for the projection based on market research. An interview with the insurance agent currently insuring the property indicated that there would be no increase in the insurance costs, and HOA documents showed there were no upcoming increases in the HOA dues.

Trash and Internet/TV expenses were included in the HOA fees, and the repairs and maintenance expenses were projected to be stable. Because the property had never been used as a short-term vacation rental, market expenses were used for administration, property listing services and management fees.

INCOME DATA

The property has not historically been used as a short-term vacation rental, so market data is required to project the ADR and Occupancy Rate. The property will be available for rent 365 days per year. Airdna data and comparable properties was used to estimate ADR and Occupancy Rates.

AVERAGE DAILY RATE:	$550
DAYS AVAILABLE:	365
PROJECTED OCCUPANCY:	70%

EXPENSE DATA

	Historical	Projected
Real Estate Taxes	$4,000	$4,120
Insurance	$2,000	$2,000
HOA Dues	$3,000	$3,000
Gas/Electric	$3,500	$3,605
Trash	$0	$0
Internet/TV	$0	$0
Repairs and Maintenance	$3,000	$3,000
Administration	$0	1.5%
Property Listing Services	$0	3%
Management Fees	$0	15%

FORMULA

Once we have our assumptions and projections estimated, we can use the following formula to estimate a capitalization rate.

FORMULA	
	AVERAGE DAILY RATE (ADR)
(X)	DAYS AVAILABLE FOR RENT
(=)	POTENTIAL GROSS INCOME
(X)	OCCUPANCY (%)
(=)	EFFECTIVE GROSS INCOME
(-)	PROJECTED OPERATING EXPENSES
(=)	PROJECTED NOI
(/)	DIVIDED BY PURCHASE PRICE
(=)	ESTIMATED CAP RATE

PROFORMA OPERATING STATEMENT

Using the preceding formula, we can now plug our assumptions into our proforma to estimate our capitalization rate. As is demonstrated in the following proforma, the estimated capitalization rate for this property is projected at 10.82%.

	PROFORMA	
	AVERAGE DAILY RATE (ADR)	$550
(x)	DAYS AVAILABLE FOR RENT	365
(=)	POTENTIAL GROSS INCOME	$200,750
(x)	OCCUPANCY (%)	70%
(=)	EFFECTIVE GROSS INCOME	$140,525
(-)	LESS PROJECTED EXPENSES	
	REAL ESTATE TAXES	$4,120
	INSURANCE	$2,000
	HOA DUES	$3,000
	GAS/ELECTRIC	$3,605
	TRASH	$0
	INTERNET/TV	$0
	REPAIRS AND MAINTENANCE	$3,000
	ADMINISTRATION (1.5% EGI)	$2,108
	PROPERTY LISTING SERVICES (3% EGI)	$4,216
	MANAGEMENT FEES (15% EGI)	$21,079
(=)	PROJECTED NOI	$97,397
(/)	DIVIDED BY PURCHASE PRICE	$900,000
(=)	ESTIMATED CAP RATE	10.82%

ADDITIONAL RESOURCES

This chapter may feel overwhelming for those new to the vacation rental game. There are indeed numerous factors to consider when conducting a financial analysis for a potential investment. However, by comprehending the fundamental aspects of valuation, you will outperform those who make emotional purchases and make more informed investment decisions. As a reminder, if you would like a **FREE** automated version of this proforma, you can find it at vacationpropertysecrets.com/freevaluationtool.

Once we have gone through our preliminary analysis as detailed throughout this chapter, we can then plug our assumption and extend our analysis over a ten-year holding period. This is where we take appreciation, inflation, and rent growth into consideration.

This is detailed modeling that is an important tool we utilize for our private equity fund. If you are interested in this advanced modeling and would like to learn more about doing this type of analysis, we offer our 10-year valuation tools in our online masterclass at vacationpropertysecrets.com/freevaluationtool.

CHAPTER 5

IDENTIFYING A HIGH-POTENTIAL MARKET

As the owner of a company specializing in managing private equity funds, I have devoted a significant portion of my efforts to identifying investment opportunities. One of the most crucial aspects of our decision-making process involves selecting high-potential markets that offer our investors the highest possible investment returns. This means having to consider numerous factors and making sure thorough due diligence is a top priority.

Unfortunately, many vacation home investors don't evaluate all the factors, but instead, base their purchases solely on emotions and personal preferences, such as the amenities available in the area or its proximity to their primary residence. While this approach may be suitable for deciding where to purchase a vacation home based on personal enjoyment, it may not align with investment goals and strategies.

If your primary intention is to spend significant time at the vacation home, and the property's revenue generation is not a crucial factor, making an emotional decision based on pure enjoyment can be reasonable.

However, if you are relying on the property's income and cash flow as a fundamental aspect, it is critical to invest the time and effort to thoroughly research the markets you are considering for purchase.

PERSONAL PREFERENCES FOR CHOOSING A LOCATION

When finding the right location for your vacation home, personal preferences as well as investment fundamental factors should be considered. And the amount of weight that should be given to each of these is highly dependent on your personal and investment goals.

For example, if you are seeking to occupy the property a considerable amount of time, you might prioritize your personal goals, while investors who are seeking to maximize their potential returns on the investment will likely focus on the investment fundamentals. Both strategies are fine, but both have to be aligned with your intentions and goals for the property.

When looking for a vacation home investment, there are a number of personal preference factors that can vary depending on your preferences, lifestyle, and goals that you should take into consideration.

Accessibility

If you plan on spending a significant amount of time at your vacation home, it is imperative that you take accessibility into consideration. Think about the frequency and ease of your visits. If the vacation home is within a few hours' drive, it can be used for weekend getaways, making it possible to enjoy the property regularly. If the property is further away, travel becomes more lengthy, and you may find yourself using it less often, primarily for longer stays or vacations.

To illustrate this point, let's consider my current situation. I reside in Denver, Colorado, which is approximately one and a half hours away from the ski areas in Summit County. While this may seem like a short distance, it can be challenging to access the property during treacherous mountain winter conditions. In such instances, having someone present in the area can be immensely beneficial if any issues arise or if weather conditions prevent access to the property.

However, the proximity does make it convenient to spend weekends or take short trips to the mountains when the property is not being rented. When we owned our slice of heaven in the mountains, we thoroughly enjoyed spending summers attending festivals, then witnessing the vibrant colors of fall foliage, and finally hitting the slopes in winter.

On the other hand, we are also purchasing properties in Costa Rica. Although Costa Rica is significantly far from our home base, Denver International Airport offers direct flights to Costa Rica, with a flight time of less than five hours. This might not be an ideal vacation home for someone seeking a quick weekend getaway, but it serves as an excellent vacation destination when we desire extended stays for weeks or even months.

The distance to your vacation home can also significantly impact property management. If the property is nearby, you can take care of cleaning, maintenance, and repairs yourself, or respond quickly if issues arise. This could potentially save you money and give you more control over the upkeep of your property.

However, if the property is far away, you may need to hire a property management service or a local caretaker. While this can add to the overall cost, it can also provide peace of mind knowing your property is well-maintained and that there's someone local who can respond to emergencies or problems.

Also, if you plan to rent out your vacation home when you're not using it, the proximity to your primary residence can affect this as well. Managing a short-term rental involves not just maintenance, but also tasks like key exchange or check-in/check-out procedures, guest communication, and troubleshooting. Again, you may need to enlist the help of a property management service if the property is far from your primary residence.

There is also the aspect of familiarity and community. If your vacation home is in a location you're already familiar with, you'll likely know the local amenities, culture, and attractions better. This can help you feel more at home when you're there and enable you to offer better advice or recommendations to your guests if you choose to rent it out.

Overall, while a distant vacation home might offer an exotic escape from daily life, a nearby one might provide more frequent respite and possibly easier management. That is why this is part of a *personal decision* and not an *investment fundamentals* decision based on how you plan to use and manage the property, your lifestyle, and your travel preferences.

Desired Lifestyle

When buying a vacation home, one significant motivation often extends beyond financial investment—it's about creating a desired lifestyle. Do you prefer a serene beachfront location, a bustling city, a mountain retreat, or a peaceful countryside? Consider the activities and amenities available in the area, such as outdoor recreation, cultural attractions, dining options, and entertainment.

This aspect of the decision-making process is deeply personal and varies greatly from individual to individual. It encompasses factors such as relaxation, adventure, family time, solitude, or socialization. A vacation home can be an avenue for enjoying your passions and interests, making treasured memories, and even creating traditions.

When considering what you want to build your lifestyle around, start by taking into consideration your hobbies and interests. If you are a skiing enthusiast, a property near the mountains may be ideal. If you love beach life and water sports, a coastal home could be your dream. Golfers might look for properties near prestigious courses, while nature lovers could prioritize homes near national parks or reserves. Your vacation home should facilitate and enhance the activities you love.

Next, think about the kind of environment and community that suits your lifestyle. Do you envision a tranquil, secluded getaway, or do you prefer being in the heart of the action with restaurants, shops, and entertainment options nearby? Do you value a close-knit community where you can form relationships with neighbors, or do you prefer a setting where you can enjoy privacy and solitude? Understanding your preferences in these areas can guide your choice of location and property type.

Also, consider your family's needs and preferences. If you have children, you might want a property with plenty of space to play, proximity to family-friendly attractions, or features like a swimming pool. If you plan to have extended family or friends visit, you might look for a home with extra bedrooms and bathrooms, a large dining area, or guest-friendly amenities.

Overall, buying a vacation home is an opportunity to pursue the lifestyle you desire by creating a space where you can enjoy your leisure time in the ways you value most. Taking the time to envision and understand what this means for you can help guide your purchasing decision and ensure you find a vacation home that brings you joy and fulfillment.

Climate and Seasonality

Another personal preference is around the climate and seasonality of the potential location. Think about the seasonality of the area and how it may impact your usage and rental potential. Do you prefer warm, sunny destinations, cooler climates, or the changing seasons?

INVESTMENT FUNDAMENTALS: RESEARCHING LOCAL REAL ESTATE MARKETS

When diving into the investment fundamentals, researching local real estate markets is of the utmost importance, which involves quite a few steps and processes.

Identifying the Target Area

Determine the specific area or region where you are interested in investing in a vacation property. This could be a particular city, town, beachfront, mountain area, or any other location that aligns with your preferences and investment goals.

Market Analysis

Conduct a thorough market analysis of the target area. Research key market indicators such as average property prices, sales trends, rental rates, occupancy rates, and market inventory. Look for data on both recent and historical trends to gain a better understanding of the market's stability and growth potential.

Local Economic Factors

Assess the local economic factors that can impact the real estate market, such as job growth, population trends, income levels, and any major industries or employers in the area. A strong and diverse local economy can contribute to a stable and desirable real estate market.

Tourism and Vacation Rental Market

Investigate the tourism industry and vacation rental market in the area. Research the number of tourists, seasonal fluctuations, popular attractions, and the demand for vacation rentals. Analyze data on occupancy rates, average rental income, and rental regulations that may apply to short-term rentals.

Infrastructure and Development

Evaluate the infrastructure and development projects in the area. Look for upcoming or planned improvements in transportation, amenities, and public facilities. These developments can positively impact property values and rental demand.

Local Regulations and Zoning

Understand the local regulations and zoning ordinances that may affect your investment. Research any restrictions on short-term rentals, property use, building codes, or any specific rules applicable to vacation properties. Ensure compliance with local laws and assess their potential impact on your investment strategy.

Network with Local Experts

Connect with local real estate agents, property managers, and industry professionals who have expertise in the target area. They can provide valuable insights, market data, and guidance based on their local knowledge and experience.

Online Resources

Leverage online resources and real estate websites to gather information on property listings, market trends, and statistics. Websites like Zillow, Realtor.com, and local Multiple Listing Services (MLS) can provide valuable data on property prices, rental rates, and market conditions.

Visit the Area

Whenever possible, visit the target area in person to gain firsthand experience and assess the surroundings. Explore the neighborhood, talk to locals, visit attractions, and get a sense of the overall ambiance. This can provide valuable insights that online research may not capture fully.

Professional Advice

Consider consulting with a real estate attorney or financial advisor who specializes in vacation property investments. They can provide guidance on legal and financial aspects specific to the target area and ensure that you make informed decisions.

Remember that real estate markets can be dynamic and subject to change, so it's important to regularly update your research and stay informed about local market conditions and trends. The more thorough and comprehensive your research, the better equipped you'll be to make informed investment decisions in the vacation property market.

SELECTING THE BEST POTENTIAL MARKETS

There are seven critical data points that our private equity fund takes into consideration when selecting a high potential market. These criteria include

- Legal and Regulatory Considerations
- Seasonality (Days Available to Rent)
- Market Amenities
- Financial Feasibility and ROIs
- Revenue Growth
- Renter Demand and Inventory
- Property Value Growth

LEGAL AND REGULATORY CONSIDERATIONS

Your first research priority is the legal and regulatory considerations for the markets you're looking at. If you're looking at a community that restricts or forbids short-term vacation rentals, you may be able to quickly eliminate that market. There are also a multitude of laws and regulations that can have an impact on your ability to rent a property to a short-term vacation tenant. When doing your research, consider the following important factors.

Zoning Laws

One of the first things you need to do when researching a market is to familiarize yourself with the local zoning laws that apply to vacation rental properties. Zoning regulations determine how properties can be used in specific areas. Some zones may have restrictions on short-term rentals or specific requirements for operating vacation rentals.

Check the local zoning code or consult with local authorities to determine if your property is zoned for short-term rentals. If the market you're considering prohibits short-term vacation rentals or has restrictions in place that don't allow renting a vacation home, you will not have revenue-generating opportunities. However, if you're simply looking for a vacation home that you're not interested in renting, a market like this would still be an option.

Permitting and Licensing

It's also important to determine if there are any permits or licenses required to legally operate a vacation rental in the area you are considering. Some jurisdictions may require specific permits or licenses, such as a vacation rental permit, business license, or transient occupancy tax (TOT) certificate. Make sure you research the application process, any associated fees, and the requirements for obtaining and renewing these permits.

Rental Duration and Minimum Stay Requirements

Some areas have regulations regarding rental duration and minimum stay requirements for vacation rentals. There may be restrictions on the number of nights a property can be rented or minimum stay requirements, such as a minimum of thirty days or more. Ensure you comply with these regulations to avoid any penalties or legal issues.

Safety and Building Codes

Develop a working knowledge of the safety and building codes applicable to vacation rental properties, and ensure that your property meets all necessary safety requirements, including fire safety measures, carbon monoxide detectors, and proper exits. Familiarize yourself with local building codes to ensure your property is compliant with any specific regulations related to vacation rentals.

Noise and Nuisance Regulations

Check for any noise and nuisance regulations that may affect your vacation rental. Some areas may have noise ordinances or quiet hours that need to be adhered to. Familiarize yourself with any restrictions on parties, events, or excessive noise that could disturb neighbors or violate local regulations.

Homeowner Association (HOA) Rules

If the property you are considering is part of a homeowner association, review the association's rules and regulations. Some HOAs have specific restrictions on vacation rentals, including rental frequency, guest behavior, or rental management requirements. Ensure that you understand and comply with these rules to maintain a good relationship with the HOA and avoid any penalties. There's nothing worse than buying a property and having to contend with an HOA that consistently makes renting your property difficult!

Taxation and Reporting Requirements

Research the taxation and reporting requirements for vacation rental properties in your area, including the local transient occupancy tax

(TOT) or lodging tax that may be applicable to short-term rentals. Then familiarize yourself with the procedures for collecting and remitting taxes to the appropriate tax authorities.

Recently, hotel owners have expressed concerns about what they perceive as an unlevel playing field when it comes to regulation and taxation of renting vacation homes, and have begun pushing for municipalities to collect taxes from vacation homeowners to level the playing field.

Hotels operate under strict regulatory requirements, including safety and health inspections, zoning regulations, and various local and state-level tax obligations. However, many vacation rental owners operate under less stringent regulations, particularly individual homeowners renting out their properties. This regulatory discrepancy can give vacation rentals a perceived advantage, as they might avoid costs and restrictions that hotels must contend with.

Additionally, there is a concern among hoteliers that some vacation rental owners may not be accurately reporting income and thus not paying their fair share of taxes. This can potentially deprive local governments of important revenue sources often derived from the hospitality industry. For these reasons, many in the hotel industry advocate for stricter regulations and enforcement for vacation rentals to ensure a more equitable marketplace.

Eviction and Guest Screening Laws

When you think about having to evict a tenant, you typically think of long-term rentals. However, it is important that you also have a good understanding of the eviction laws as they relate to your vacation home. Eviction laws and guest screening procedures for short-term vacation rentals can be complex and vary significantly by location.

Regarding evictions, owners of vacation rentals must adhere to local laws and ordinances that govern the process. If a guest overstays their rental period or violates the rental agreement in some way, the property owner typically cannot immediately evict them without following legal procedures. These procedures can include giving a notice to vacate and filing an eviction lawsuit. Some areas may even have special protections in place for short-term tenants that could further complicate the eviction process. It's crucial for property owners to familiarize themselves with local laws to ensure they handle such situations legally and ethically.

For guest screening, while property owners do have some leeway to establish their criteria, they must still abide by federal, state, and local laws that prohibit discrimination. For instance, in the United States, the Fair Housing Act prohibits discrimination based on race, color, national origin, religion, sex, familial status, or disability. Other countries have similar laws. Some platforms like Airbnb also have policies against discrimination. Moreover, while property owners can (and should) screen potential guests for factors like past reviews, verified identities, and agreement to house rules, they can't refuse a booking based on discriminatory reasons. It's essential for property owners to conduct their screening processes in a way that respects the rights of all potential guests. These laws and regulations are designed to ensure fairness and protect the rights of both parties in the vacation rental process.

Grandfather Clauses

When looking into the zoning and restrictions in a market, there may be opportunities to purchase a property that has a transferable license in place which would allow you to continue using the property as a vacation rental. Because some properties are "grandfathered" in, use as a short-term rental is potentially possible even though the community may now be restricting this property use type.

A "grandfather clause" in the context of short-term vacation rentals refers to a provision that exempts certain properties from new zoning rules or regulations based on the fact that they were in existence before these new rules were implemented.

However, these grandfather clauses can come with conditions. For instance, they might only apply as long as the property continues to be used for the same purpose and does not undergo significant changes. If the property is sold, the new owner may not be able to continue operating under the same grandfathered terms. Additionally, if the property is not used as a short-term rental for a certain period, it may lose its grandfathered status.

It's important to note that not all jurisdictions will offer grandfather clauses when new laws are passed. Property owners should stay informed about local regulations and consider legal advice if necessary.

It is essential to consult with local authorities, such as the planning department, city or county officials, or a real estate attorney, to obtain accurate and up-to-date information regarding local zoning and regulations for vacation rental properties. Non-compliance with local regulations can result in fines, legal issues, and reputational damage, so it's crucial to understand and adhere to the applicable rules and requirements.

SEASONALITY

Seasonality, the days available to rent, plays a significant role in the success and profitability of vacation home rentals. The demand for vacation rentals can fluctuate dramatically based on the time of year, which directly influences rental rates and occupancy levels.

For instance, a beachfront property is likely to be in high demand during the summer months, allowing for higher rental rates and nearly continuous occupancy. Conversely, during the off-peak season, demand may decline significantly, leading to lower rental rates and potentially long periods without guests. The same holds true for a mountain property that tends to be in high demand during the ski season and has lower occupancy during the summer months and virtually no occupancy during the spring and fall seasons.

It's not just about the weather, though. Local events and attractions also contribute to the seasonality of vacation home rentals. Properties in areas with popular winter activities like skiing or holiday markets may see a spike in demand during the colder months. Locations known for annual events, festivals, or conventions can also experience increased demand during those times.

However, the off-season for these properties could mean lower income and potential vacancies. Thus, understanding the seasonality of your location is vital when forecasting potential rental income and managing expenses. Property owners often need to budget carefully to ensure they can cover costs during slower periods. Some may even adjust their marketing strategies throughout the year, promoting different amenities or local attractions that might appeal to guests in each season, to maximize their rental's appeal year-round.

MARKET AMENITIES

Researching amenities in a market for short-term vacation rentals is an essential step in maximizing your property's appeal and potential profitability. Amenities refer not only to the features within your property (like a pool, fireplace, high-speed internet, or a well-equipped kitchen), but also to the attractions and services in the surrounding area, such as restaurants, parks, entertainment venues, shopping centers, and public transportation access.

Start by considering your target guest demographic. For example, families with children might appreciate the proximity to parks, beaches, or family-friendly attractions, while business travelers may value a quiet workspace, fast internet, and easy access to public transportation.

Conducting a thorough competitor analysis can also provide insights into the most sought-after amenities in your market.

Look at other successful rentals in your area, noting the amenities they offer and the reviews they receive. Guest reviews often highlight the amenities that were particularly appreciated or those that were missed.

A detailed understanding of your market's amenities can help inform your property investment and management strategies. It may guide decisions about renovations or improvements to your property, the kind of services you might want to offer (like bike rentals or grocery delivery), and how you market your property.

For example, if your property is in a location renowned for its hiking trails, you might highlight this in your listing and provide amenities such as trail maps, hiking gear storage, or a hot tub for post-hike relaxation. Properly leveraging the unique amenities of your market can set your vacation rental apart and enhance its appeal to potential guests.

FINANCIAL FEASIBILITY AND ROIS

The purchase price of a vacation rental property plays a crucial role in determining the return on investment (ROI). ROI is a key financial metric used to measure the probability or success of an investment and is typically expressed as a percentage. When it comes to vacation rental properties, ROI can be calculated by dividing the property's annual net profit by its purchase price.

The higher the purchase price of a property, the higher the annual net profit needs to be to achieve a good ROI. For instance, if you purchase a property for a high price in a prime location, you'd need to command high rental rates and maintain consistent occupancy to offset the high initial investment and earn a strong return. Additionally, more expensive properties often come with higher ongoing costs such as property taxes, insurance, and maintenance costs, which could further eat into your profits.

On the other hand, purchasing a property at a lower price point can potentially offer a better ROI, even if it commands lower rental rates. This is because the initial investment is lower, and ongoing costs are likely to be less as well. However, properties with lower purchase prices may be located in less popular areas, making it harder to attract guests and maintain consistent occupancy.

Therefore, when considering the purchase price of a vacation rental property, it is important to also consider its potential for rental income and the associated ongoing costs. A property with a high purchase price might offer high rental income potential, but it could also come with high ongoing costs that could reduce your net profit and ROI. Similarly, a property with a low purchase price might offer less rental income potential, but also less ongoing costs, potentially leading to a better net profit and ROI.

It's also important to remember that property value appreciation can contribute to ROI. Even if a property doesn't offer a high immediate return through rental income, it could still be a good investment if property values in the area are rising and you can sell the property for a significant profit in the future. As with any investment, it's important to conduct thorough research and possibly consult with a real estate professional before making a decision.

When we launched the Blue Fusion private equity fund, one of the markets I was most interested in was Manhattan Beach, California because it is a place I really enjoy spending time, and the area offers many of the amenities and activities important to me. It is also the spot I can go to have my favorite beer and wings at my favorite restaurant. To say I was extremely excited at the prospect is an understatement!

The nightly rental rates were high in this market (good), but the purchase prices and expenses associated with the property were even higher (not good). This market was not an area that could get us the returns we had targeted for our investors. I, of course, was disappointed with these results, but as I mentioned before, to be successful it is important to buy based on the fundamentals and not emotional attachments.

Just because an area has high rental rates does not mean it will provide the returns you're looking for. Conversely, just because an area may be inexpensive to buy in does not mean that it will generate the rental rates needed to get a good ROI. Affordability is not about price, but about being able to buy a property that generates enough ROI to provide the rate of return that meets your expectations.

REVENUE GROWTH

Analyzing rental rate growth is crucial for optimizing the performance and profitability of your short-term vacation rental. Understanding how rental rates fluctuate and grow over time can inform your pricing strategies, help you anticipate market trends, and ultimately enhance your return on investment.

When doing your market research, start by examining historical rental rates for similar properties in your area. This can give you a sense of how rates have evolved over time, as well as seasonal trends. You may notice that rates rise during peak travel seasons and fall during off-peak periods. You might also see longer-term trends, such as steadily rising rates over several years. Analyzing these patterns can help you forecast future rental rate growth and set competitive prices for your property. There are also resources such as AirDNA that provide good historical data on rental rate growth in specific markets.

It is also important to stay abreast of factors that could impact future rental rate growth. This can include changes in local tourism trends, new amenities or attractions in the area, and changes in local laws or regulations. For instance, if a major new attraction is opening in your area, it could drive up demand for vacation rentals and allow for higher rental rates. On the other hand, if new regulations restrict short-term rentals, it could reduce demand and limit rental rate growth.

If you do not want to spend money on a resource such as AirDNA, you can leverage online platforms like Airbnb and VRBO that provide useful data for analyzing rental rate growth. You can also reach out to local tourism boards or real estate agencies to get an idea of what is happening in the markets you are considering. There are also a number of property management software companies with expertise in dynamic pricing strategies which adjust rental rates in real time based on factors like demand, seasonality, and local market conditions.

RENTER DEMAND AND INVENTORY

It is important to look at the demand for short-term rental properties in the markets you are considering, as well as the inventory available to fulfill the needs of vacationers. Understanding the ebb and flow of rental demand in a given location can offer valuable insights into the potential profitability of your investment and help shape your rental strategy.

There are several ways to gauge rental demand. Start by examining occupancy rates for existing vacation rentals in your targeted area. Many online platforms, like Airbnb or VRBO, display calendar availability which can provide a snapshot of how often properties are booked. A high occupancy rate is typically a good indication of strong demand. However, remember that these rates can fluctuate significantly throughout the year, so it is important to analyze data from all seasons to get a comprehensive understanding.

In addition to occupancy rates, look at local tourism trends. High levels of tourist traffic can suggest strong demand for vacation rentals. Local tourism boards often provide statistics on visitor numbers, and you can also look at factors like the number of nearby attractions, events, and amenities that might draw tourists to the area.

It is also beneficial to consider broader demographic and economic trends. For example, a location with a growing population, strong job growth, or plans for major development projects might see increased demand for rentals in the future.

Furthermore, seek to understand the unique factors that might affect demand in your targeted location. For example, if the area is known for a specific event or season (like a music festival or ski season), demand might be particularly high during those times.

Analyzing the rental demand for your market is a multi-faceted process that requires a deep understanding of both the local characteristics and broader trends. By conducting thorough market research, you can make informed decisions about where to invest in a vacation rental and how to position your property for success.

PROPERTY VALUE GROWTH

Another important factor to consider when selecting the location of an investment is property value growth potential. Buying a short-term vacation home is an investment, and the best rate of return occurs on properties in markets that have good appreciation. An appreciation in property values can contribute significantly to the return on investment, alongside rental income. A healthy growth rate can also provide a safety net, in the event you decide to sell the property in the future.

When doing your research, start by looking through online real estate platforms, local realtor associations, or county records for historical home price data for the area you're interested in. As you review the trends over time, take note of how home prices have fluctuated. A steady upward trend suggests consistent property value growth, while sudden spikes or drops could signal market instability.

To ensure you review trends over a typical full real estate cycle, be sure to look at a ten-year period. Looking at a partial cycle could skew your results and cause you to overestimate or underestimate your projected appreciation rate.

It is also beneficial to analyze the factors driving property value growth. A region experiencing economic growth, job creation, and population influx is more likely to have sustained property value appreciation. Local factors such as new developments, infrastructure improvements, school district ratings, and changes in zoning laws can also impact property values.

Keep an eye on the future prospects of the area as well. Are there plans for major developments that could boost property values? Are there potential risks such as changes in local regulations or environmental hazards that could negatively impact values?

And finally, you should take into consideration the unique characteristics of individual properties. Factors like the condition of the property, its size and layout, its proximity to amenities, and its potential for upgrades or renovations can all affect its value growth.

Doing market research and understanding property value growth trends not only helps in making an informed buying decision but also allows you to forecast potential future returns. But always remember, while past performance is a useful indicator, it does not guarantee future results, so it is important to continually monitor market conditions and adjust your strategies accordingly.

LOCATION SELECTION CASE STUDY

For practice and clarity of all we've discussed, we will look at a case study considering two potential markets to purchase a short-term vacation home investment. Both markets are located in California; however, one of the markets is a beach community in southern California, and the other is centrally located in the desert in an area frequently visited by people looking to get out of the urban areas.

BEACH PROPERTY

The beach property has the following locational attributes.

Zoning and Regulatory Considerations

Short-term vacation rentals are allowed in this community, and it is a place tourists like to visit. There are also no restrictions on the number of nights renters are allowed to stay, and owners are allowed to use the property as a short-term vacation rental year-round.

Seasonality (Days Available to Rent)

The high season for beach rentals in Southern California generally spans from late spring to early fall. The high season tends to coincide with the warmest months of the year, offering ideal beach weather for visitors.

Beaches are often bustling with tourists and vacationers seeking to enjoy the region's sunny weather, warm temperatures, and coastal attractions. Because its peak season aligns with school vacations, summer holidays, and popular events, the area attracts a significant influx of visitors.

Market Amenities

There are many market amenities related to typical beach activities (swimming, surfing, volleyball, etc.). In addition, the area has a significant number of restaurants offering a wide range of prices and options and boasts an excellent shopping experience with a number of boutiques, local shops, and beach-related offerings. There are even recreational activities in the area, such as golfing, sailing, and deep-sea fishing. Overall, the amenities in the area are exceptional.

Financial Feasibility and ROIs

The cost of properties is very high in the area. It is important to do a projected income and expenses analysis on properties to see if they meet the investment criteria and goals.

Revenue Growth

Based on market data, revenue growth has been relatively good and is generally increasing.

Renter Demand and Inventory

Based on market data, renter demand has been high in the area, which is primarily attributed to the amenities offered in the area. However, there is also a large supply of inventory which is keeping rental rates lower due to the added competition.

Property Value Growth

Property value growth (appreciation) has been high over the last five years; however, interest rates have been climbing and recent average property values have been steady and even slightly declining in the area.

DESERT PROPERTY

The Desert property has the following locational attributes.

Zoning and Regulatory Considerations

Short-term vacation rentals are allowed in this community, and it is a place tourists like to visit. There are also no restrictions on the number of nights renters are allowed to stay, and owners are allowed to use the property as a short-term vacation rental year-round. There has been talk about potentially putting restrictions on short-term rentals in the market, but homes already being used for this purpose would be grandfathered in.

Seasonality (Days Available to Rent)

The high season for vacation home rentals in the central California desert typically occurs during the winter months, specifically from January to March. This period attracts a significant number of visitors seeking to escape colder climates and enjoy the pleasant weather and recreational activities in the Palm Desert area. The warm temperatures, sunny days, and the opportunity to engage in outdoor activities like golfing and hiking make this area a popular destination during this time.

Market Amenities

The desert area offers an array of shopping experiences, with upscale retail centers featuring a mix of high-end boutiques, designer stores, and specialty shops. The culinary scene is equally impressive, with many different dining options. The area also hosts farmers' markets with artisanal products and locally crafted goods, and has world-class golf courses and country clubs for golf enthusiasts. And the many festivals that happen during the high season in this area attract a high number of visitors.

Financial Feasibility and ROIs

The cost of properties is moderate in the area, and rental rates are relatively good. However, it is still important to do a projected income and expenses analysis on properties to see if they meet the investment criteria and goals.

Revenue Growth

Based on market data, revenue growth has been relatively good and generally increasing.

Renter Demand and Inventory

Based on market data, renter demand has been high in the area. This is primarily attributed to the amenities being offered in the area. There is also good demand in the area and a shortage of vacation homes in comparison to the demand.

Property Value Growth

Property value growth (appreciation) has been high over the last five years; however, interest rates have been climbing and recent average property values have been steady. There have not been any declines in the market as of this analysis.

MARKET COMPARISON

MARKET COMPARATION		
	BEACH	**DESERT**
ZONING AND REGULATORY	[+]	[+]
SEASONALITY	[+]	[+]
MARKET AMENITIES	[+]	[+]
FEASIBILITY AND ROI	[-]	[+]
REVENUE GROWTH	[+]	[+]
DEMAND/INVENTORY	[-]	[-]
PROPERTY VALUE GROWTH	[-]	[=]

The following shows a comparison of the two potential markets:

Both sample markets are attractive and highly sought-after areas; however, the beach area has some questions that need to be answered in regard to the potential returns and the feasibility of investing in the market. Because of the uncertainty, it is prudent to do the due diligence and run comparable cash flows for the two markets.

Financial Analysis

To conduct a financial analysis, identify a potential vacation home for sale in the area that you would be interested in purchasing and go through the valuation techniques learned earlier in this book to estimate a projected NOI.

Beach Property

The following is the analysis for the beach area property.

FOR SALE: $2,500,000

BEDROOMS:	4 Bedroom	ADR:	$782
BATHROOMS:	4 Bathrooms	OCCUPANCY:	62%
SLEEPS:	10 People	REVENUE:	$176,967

GROSS REVENUE	$176,967	
(LESS) FIXED EXPENSES	$12,500	
(LESS) VARIABLE EXPENSES	$45,000	
PROJECTED NOI	$119,467	**4.78%**
DIVIDED BY PURCHASE PRICE	$2,500,000	
ESTIMATED CAP RATE	4.78%	

Once this financial analysis was completed, we estimated the return on investment in this community to be around 5% +/-. This estimate does not include potential market appreciation but does provide a good estimate of the investment fundamentals and expectations for this market.

Desert Property

The following is the analysis for the desert area property.

FOR SALE: $950,000			
BEDROOMS:	4 Bedroom	**ADR:**	$678
BATHROOMS:	4 Bathrooms	**OCCUPANCY:**	67%
SLEEPS:	10 People	**REVENUE:**	$165,805
GROSS REVENUE	$165,805		
(LESS) FIXED EXPENSES	$12,000		
(LESS) VARIABLE EXPENSES	$40,000	**11.98%**	
PROJECTED NOI	$113,805		
DIVIDED BY PURCHASE PRICE	$950,000		
ESTIMATED CAP RATE	11.98%		

Once this financial analysis was completed, we estimated that the return on investment in this community is around 10% +/-. Again, this estimate does not include potential market appreciation but does provide a good estimate of the investment fundamentals and expectations for this market.

Based on the preceding analysis, the desert market yields better return fundamentals; however, if your buying decisions were based on more than just your expected rate of return, you could still take both markets into consideration. As an investor who is looking for better returns, I would focus my energies on the desert market due to the potential returns I could expect.

CHAPTER 6

FINDING THE PERFECT PROPERTY

I n the previous chapter, we spoke about the locational attributes you should take into consideration when searching for a vacation home. In this chapter, we will focus on the property itself and the characteristics you should consider when searching for the perfect piece of real estate. However, don't forget that the building characteristics of the perfect vacation home ultimately should also be dependent on your personal preferences and how you intend to use the property.

HOME SIZE

When buying a vacation home as a short-term rental investment, the size of the home plays a significant role in its potential profitability and appeal to renters. To determine the right size for your investment property, there are several factors you should evaluate.

First is the target rental market. If the home is in an area popular with families, a larger home with multiple bedrooms and bathrooms may be more desirable. On the other hand, if the property is in a destination more popular with couples or smaller groups, a smaller, cozier home might be a better fit.

The rental rates you can charge typically increase with the size of the home. Larger homes often bring in higher rental income per stay because they can accommodate more guests. However, larger homes also tend to have higher purchase prices and ongoing costs for maintenance, utilities, and cleaning. You'll need to evaluate whether the potential for higher rental income outweighs these additional costs.

Consider the frequency of rentals as well. Larger homes, especially those with unique features like a large outdoor space or a game room, might be rented less frequently but for longer periods, such as a week or more. Smaller homes, particularly those in urban areas, might attract shorter but more frequent stays.

The maintenance and upkeep of the property should also be taken into account. Larger homes can require more time and effort to maintain, especially if they have features like a large yard or a pool. This can lead to higher property management costs if you're not managing the property yourself.

The local real estate market is another factor to consider. Larger homes may appreciate in value more slowly than smaller homes, especially if the demand for larger vacation rentals is lower in the area. However, in a high-demand area, a larger home might be a more attractive investment because of its potential for higher rental income and property appreciation.

Finally, consider the potential for multi-purpose use. If you plan to use the home yourself in addition to renting it out, ensure it is big enough to accommodate your personal needs as well. The goal is to strike a balance between profitability, manageability, and personal enjoyment.

KITCHEN CONSIDERATIONS

The kitchen is a significant feature that can greatly impact the desirability and functionality of the property for potential renters. Consider the kitchen's size and layout in relation to the overall property. If you're investing in a larger vacation home aimed at families or large groups, a spacious and well-equipped kitchen can be a major selling point. On the contrary, if you're looking at a smaller property meant for couples or solo travelers, a compact but functional kitchen might be sufficient.

For example, we recently purchased a four-bedroom home in Costa Rica. Due to the size of this home, it appeals to multiple families. With this home, there is a large kitchen and living area with floor-to-ceiling doors extending twenty feet and opening up to the outside grilling area, patio, and pool. As you can imagine, this is an area where families can get together to cook, relax, and enjoy the infinity pool.

Additionally, the kitchen's functionality is crucial. Ensure it is equipped with the necessary appliances like a stove, oven, microwave, dishwasher, and a good-sized refrigerator. Renters on vacation are likely to value the convenience these provide, even if they don't plan on cooking large meals. Additionally, easy-to-clean surfaces can reduce cleaning time and cost between guests.

The condition and age of the appliances and fixtures should also be considered. While slightly older appliances might still be functional, newer ones often offer better energy efficiency, which can save on utility costs in the long run. They can also be more appealing to potential renters.

Consider the ease of use for your potential guests. A well-stocked kitchen with basics such as pots, pans, utensils, a coffee maker, and a toaster can make the stay more comfortable for your guests. The more at home your guests feel, the higher the chance they might leave a positive review, leading to more bookings in the future.

The aesthetic appeal of the kitchen is also important. Light, bright, and modern kitchens often photograph well, which can make your listing more attractive. Consider the style and colors in the kitchen and how they fit with the overall aesthetic of the property.

Finally, it is beneficial to consider the return on investment for any potential upgrades to the kitchen. While a full remodel might significantly increase the property's appeal, it can also be costly. Determine whether the potential increase in rental income and property value is likely to offset the cost of any upgrades.

THE BEDROOMS

When looking at the bedroom configurations in a short-term vacation rental, the number, size, and layout of the bedrooms can significantly impact the appeal of your property to potential renters.

First and foremost, consider the number of bedrooms in relation to the target market for your rental. If you are catering to families or large groups, a property with multiple bedrooms would likely be more desirable. Conversely, if your potential renters are mainly couples or solo travelers, a one or two-bedroom property might suffice. The number of bedrooms can also directly affect your rental rates, as properties with more bedrooms typically command higher prices.

The layout and size of the bedrooms are important considerations as well. Bedrooms should be large enough to comfortably accommodate guests and their belongings. Consider if the bedrooms offer enough privacy for guests, especially in larger homes that might be rented by multiple families or groups of friends. Ensuring each room feels private and comfortable can increase the appeal of your property.

Many homes are now offering two primary bedrooms, which would appeal to multiple families seeking to rent the property. When there is a single primary bedroom in place, everyone wants it. However, two primary bedrooms would be ideal for two families with two sets of parents who each have their own primary, and smaller second and third bedrooms for the children.

The bedrooms' positioning within the house is another aspect to take into account. If the property is multi-leveled, consider the distribution of the bedrooms. A property with a primary bedroom on the main level and additional bedrooms upstairs or downstairs might appeal to families with older relatives or those with young children.

Consider the potential for flexible sleeping arrangements. Having bedrooms that can accommodate different configurations (for example, twin beds that can be pushed together or a king bed that can be split into two singles) can make your property more versatile and appealing to a wider range of guests.

Ensuite bathrooms can be a big draw for vacation rentals, adding convenience and a sense of luxury. If the property doesn't have ensuites for all bedrooms, make sure there are sufficient bathrooms in convenient locations relative to the bedrooms.

Finally, consider the overall atmosphere and decor of the bedrooms. A vacation home should feel like a retreat, so bedrooms should provide a relaxing, tranquil environment. Good lighting, comfortable mattresses, ample storage for clothes and luggage, and a pleasing aesthetic can all contribute to positive guest experiences.

There is nothing worse than checking into a vacation home and finding uncomfortable beds and pillows. Your renters are there to relax and recover from their day-to-day lives. Give them an experience that will keep them returning to your property! Catering to the needs and expectations of your target rental market can help to ensure your property is competitive and profitable.

BATHROOMS

Bathrooms play a key role in the overall comfort and appeal of a short-term vacation rental property. The number, size, design, and amenities of the bathrooms can significantly influence a potential renter's decision.

Take into consideration the number of bathrooms relative to the number of bedrooms. As a general rule, having at least one bathroom for every two bedrooms is a good ratio. This ensures guests won't have to wait too long to use the facilities, particularly during peak times in the morning and evening. However, the better the ratio, the more appealing the house. Kids can generally share a bathroom relatively easily, but couples staying at the property will usually want their own.

If the property is large and caters to big groups, having multiple bathrooms or even ensuites can be a huge selling point. Ensuite bathrooms add a level of convenience and luxury that many renters appreciate, especially in a group setting where privacy can be highly valued.

The size and layout of the bathrooms are also important. A bathroom should be spacious enough to comfortably accommodate the guests. Consider the ease of movement within the bathroom, the amount of counter space available, and the adequacy of storage for toiletries.

Another aspect to consider is the fixtures and amenities within the bathrooms. Most renters expect to find all the usual fixtures like a sink, toilet, and shower or bathtub. However, additional features like double sinks, a walk-in shower, or a soaking tub can significantly enhance a bathroom's appeal.

Also, look at the condition of the bathrooms. Outdated or poorly maintained bathrooms can detract from the overall appeal of the property. Even if the rest of the home is up to par, a dilapidated bathroom can be a deal-breaker for many potential renters.

Finally, consider the style and decor of the bathrooms. Just like other parts of the property, the bathrooms should offer a pleasing aesthetic.

Consider whether the style of the bathrooms matches the overall style of the property and whether any upgrades or renovations might be needed to improve their appearance.

Ensuring the bathrooms meet the needs and expectations of your target rental market can help to maximize the appeal and profitability of your property.

INDOOR LIVING SPACES

The indoor living spaces, including the living room, dining area, and any additional entertainment spaces, play a critical role in the property's overall appeal. These areas often serve as the focal point of the rental experience where guests relax, dine, and socialize. Therefore, it is crucial to carefully evaluate these spaces when considering a potential investment property.

The size and layout of the living spaces should be proportional to the rest of the property. A larger property designed to accommodate multiple guests or families should have ample living space to comfortably host everyone. Similarly, a smaller property aimed at couples, or solo travelers should have cozy, inviting living spaces that enhance the homey feel.

Comfort is key when it comes to indoor living spaces. Consider the quality of the furniture, particularly the sofas and chairs. Seating should be ample and comfortable, and the layout should facilitate conversation. A well-positioned television, a sound system, or a game console could add to the appeal, particularly for longer stays or during times of inclement weather.

The aesthetics of the living space also matter. The decor and style should match the overall theme of the property and appeal to the target market. Remember, the first impression of your property often comes from the photos in the listing, and the living room is usually one of the featured images.

In the dining area, consider the size and number of seats, as it should be able to comfortably seat the maximum number of guests the property can accommodate. The availability of additional seating, like a breakfast bar or an outdoor dining set, can be an added advantage.

If the property has additional entertainment spaces, such as a game room, a home theater, or a reading nook, it will be even more appealing to many renters. These amenities can differentiate your property from others and justify a higher rental rate.

Lighting in the living spaces can also greatly affect the atmosphere. Natural light is usually preferable, but well-planned artificial lighting can also create a pleasant ambiance.

Also take into consideration the potential maintenance requirements of the living spaces. High-traffic areas can wear out quickly, so durable, easy-to-clean furnishings and finishes might be a wise choice. A well-designed and appealing living space can enhance the guest experience, leading to positive reviews and repeat bookings, thereby maximizing your rental income.

HOME AMENITIES

When considering home amenities, start with the WiFi, air conditioning, heating, and laundry facilities. These are often considered essential by travelers. A reliable, high-speed internet connection is particularly important, as many guests will want to stream movies or may need to work remotely during their stay. Depending on your location, effective heating and/or air conditioning systems can make the difference between a comfortable and an uncomfortable stay.

Next, evaluate the kitchen. Many guests prefer vacation rentals over hotels because they offer the opportunity to cook meals. A well-equipped kitchen with modern appliances, cookware, utensils, and a good amount of workspace can be a major selling point. Consider including a dishwasher for added convenience.

Bathroom amenities are also crucial. Adequate water pressure, plentiful hot water, and modern fixtures can enhance guests' comfort. Providing basics such as towels, toilet paper, and a hairdryer can also be appreciated by guests.

Another aspect that can boost the appeal of your property is entertainment amenities. This might include things like a flat-screen TV with access to streaming services, a stereo system, board games, or books. If your property is family-friendly, consider including amenities for children, such as toys or a crib.

Outdoor amenities can be another draw, especially in locations with good weather. This could include a barbecue grill, outdoor seating or dining areas, a fire pit, a pool, or sports equipment like bicycles or beach gear.

Lastly, consider any unique amenities that could set your property apart. This might be a hot tub, a game room, a home gym, or a well-stocked library. While not necessarily essential, these unique touches can make your property stand out in the vacation rental market and create memorable experiences for your guests.

STORAGE AREAS

When purchasing a short-term vacation rental property, storage spaces may not be the first thing on your mind; however, they play a vital role in enhancing the comfort and convenience of your guests' stay.

Bedrooms should ideally have closets large enough to accommodate clothing and personal items for the length of a typical stay. And closets in the main living areas are useful for storing games, toys, or additional linens and pillows.

In addition to regular closets, consider the availability and location of larger storage spaces. If your vacation home is in a location that lends itself to outdoor activities like skiing, biking, or beach-going, guests will appreciate a place to store their gear. This might be a garage, a mudroom, a secure outdoor shed, or even a large closet.

For example, when we purchased our ski cabin in Keystone, Colorado, one of the most valuable spaces was the ski and snowboard closet located just outside the front door. It made it easy for the family to sit on the bench next to the closet, remove ski gear, and store it until the next day of hitting the slopes.

The kitchen is another area where ample storage is important. Guests should have enough space to store groceries, especially if they plan on cooking during their stay. Additionally, having a place to store smaller appliances when not in use can keep counters clear and the kitchen looking tidy.

Consider, too, the storage needs of the property itself. If you're providing items like beach chairs, barbecue equipment, bicycles, or outdoor games, you'll need a place to store these when not in use. This is particularly important in off-season periods when these items might not be used for several months.

When evaluating a property, consider whether the existing storage spaces are sufficient or if there is the potential to add more. Adding storage can sometimes be a relatively minor renovation that significantly enhances the functionality and appeal of the property. By ensuring your property has sufficient storage, you can ensure your guests have a comfortable, convenient stay, which can lead to positive reviews and repeat bookings.

OUTDOOR LIVING SPACES

The outdoor living spaces of a short-term vacation rental property can be a significant draw for potential guests, especially if your property is in a region with favorable weather. These spaces can serve as areas for relaxation, dining, and entertainment.

Consider the size and layout of the outdoor space. Whether it is a balcony, patio, or sprawling backyard, it should be proportional to the size of the property and the number of guests it can accommodate. A larger property meant for families or group rentals might benefit from a substantial outdoor area with multiple seating and dining options, while a smaller property aimed at couples, or solo travelers might only require a cozy patio or balcony.

The functionality of the outdoor space is another critical factor. Consider if it is equipped with suitable outdoor furniture, a BBQ grill, a fire pit, or even an outdoor kitchen. These amenities can significantly enhance the appeal of your property, providing guests with unique dining and relaxation options.

Our most recent purchase in Costa Rica features an outdoor kitchen that allows families to spend their time out on the expansive patio by the pool, overlooking the ocean, enjoying grilling and relaxing. It is an impressive selling point for the property.

Outdoor spaces should also offer a certain level of privacy. Whether this is achieved through fencing, strategic landscaping, or the property's location, guests will appreciate a space where they can unwind without feeling watched.

If your property has a swimming pool, hot tub, or other water features, consider the upkeep these will require. They can be a strong selling point for guests, but they also involve additional maintenance and can increase insurance costs. Also, safety features like gates or alarms for pools should be considered, especially if your potential guests include families with children.

The landscaping of the property is another aspect to take into account. While beautiful landscaping can enhance curb appeal and create an inviting outdoor space, it can also entail additional maintenance. Opt for landscaping that complements the local climate to minimize water usage and upkeep.

Additionally, consider the view from the outdoor space. A property with a beautiful view can often command higher rental rates. If the property doesn't have a view, consider how you might create a visually pleasing outdoor environment through landscaping or other outdoor features.

By creating a comfortable and inviting outdoor space, you can enhance the guest experience, increase your rental appeal, and potentially command higher rental rates.

LAUNDRY AREA

The availability and convenience of a laundry area is an important factor to consider. While it might not be the first thing prospective guests look for, having in-unit laundry facilities can greatly enhance the appeal and functionality of your property.

Properties that offer guests the ability to wash and dry their clothes can be more appealing, particularly for longer stays. This amenity gives guests the flexibility to pack lighter, wash their clothes after engaging in outdoor activities, or handle any unexpected spills or stains.

The location of the laundry area within the property is another consideration. It should ideally be in a convenient and discreet location. Guests typically prefer laundry facilities that are accessible but out of the way from primary living areas. A laundry closet in a hallway or a dedicated laundry room near the bedrooms are commonly preferred placements. If the property has multiple levels, consider the convenience of hauling laundry to and from the facilities.

Storage space in the laundry area is another feature to consider. A laundry area with storage for detergents, fabric softeners, and other supplies is more convenient for guests. If space allows, you might also consider providing an iron and ironing board. I personally am an ironing freak. I am always disappointed when I travel somewhere that does not have an iron and ironing board.

By providing convenient and efficient laundry facilities, you can enhance your property's appeal and improve the overall guest experience.

AMENITIES

It is also important to consider the property's proximity and access to local amenities. We spoke about the importance of selecting a market, but where the house is located in the market can have an impact on your rental rates. This aspect not only impacts your guests' experience but also the rental overall.

Make sure you are taking note of the property's proximity to key attractions in the area. This might include beaches, national parks, tourist sites, or ski resorts, depending on the location. Properties within walking distance or a short drive from major attractions are often highly sought after by vacationers.

For example, our Keystone cabin was not located on the slopes (which would command a premium), but it was located adjacent to the free shuttle that took our guests directly to and from the ski area. Renters did not have to pay the premium rental rate to be ski-in and ski-out, but they also did not need to load up their car and drive to the overcrowded parking lot, find a space, and then make their way to the base of the mountain.

Next, consider access to everyday amenities such as grocery stores, restaurants, and shops. Even while on vacation, guests will appreciate the convenience of being able to easily procure supplies, dine out, or indulge in a bit of shopping. Proximity to a town or city center can be a major selling point.

If your potential rental property is in a rural or secluded area, consider how this could impact your guests' access to amenities. While some guests might appreciate the peace and tranquility, others might find it inconvenient to drive long distances for food, entertainment, or other needs.

Public transportation can be another key consideration, particularly in urban areas or places where parking is scarce or expensive. A rental property near a subway station, bus stop, or other transit hubs can be a major asset.

Access to outdoor activities and sports facilities can also be a draw for many guests. Proximity to hiking trails, golf courses, tennis courts, or watersports rentals can enhance your property's appeal to guests who enjoy active holidays.

It is essential to consider the property's location relative to key attractions, everyday amenities, outdoor activities, and essential services when making your investment decision. By doing so, you can ensure your property offers the convenience and features that prospective guests are looking for, helping to increase occupancy rates and maximize rental income.

HOME STYLE

The style of a short-term vacation rental property can greatly influence its attractiveness to potential renters and, in turn, impact its profitability. As you consider buying a vacation home investment, here are some factors to take into account regarding the home's style.

It is important to consider the general aesthetics of the property. Is it modern, rustic, traditional, or beach-themed? The style should be fitting with the location and appeal to the types of guests you aim to attract. For instance, a beach-themed style may be appropriate for a property near the coast, while a rustic, cabin-like style would suit a mountain retreat. The aesthetic should feel cohesive throughout the home, as this can create a more pleasing and immersive experience for guests.

Think about the layout and design of the home. Open concept living spaces are popular and can make the home feel larger and more inviting. Good flow between indoor and outdoor spaces is also a plus, particularly in regions with pleasant weather. Additionally, consider the number and configuration of bedrooms and bathrooms; a property with multiple bedrooms and bathrooms may be more appealing to families or groups.

The home's style should also cater to its functionality as a vacation rental. Durable materials and finishes in high-traffic areas such as the kitchen and living room are essential. Similarly, easily cleanable surfaces and stain-resistant fabrics can help maintain the property's appearance over time and reduce maintenance effort.

When it comes to the exterior, style is important. The home should have curb appeal, which can be influenced by its architecture, color scheme, and landscaping. A well-maintained exterior not only makes a good first impression but may also be a requirement if the property is located within a homeowner's association.

Remember, the style of your vacation rental property also needs to be reflected in your online listing's photos and description. High-quality, professional photos that accurately showcase the property's style and amenities can help draw potential renters. A clear and engaging description that highlights the home's unique style and features can further increase its appeal.

MAINTENANCE CONSIDERATIONS

When identifying the perfect property, you need to understand and prepare for the maintenance needs as they can significantly impact your time, budget, and the overall profitability of your investment.

Evaluate the current condition of the property prior to making your purchase. An inspection prior to purchase can provide valuable insights into any immediate repairs or updates needed, as well as the overall quality of the property's construction and prior maintenance. High-quality construction and regular maintenance can reduce the frequency and cost of future repairs.

Consider the property's age and the lifespan of major systems and appliances. Older properties or those with older systems and appliances may require more frequent repairs or replacements. The HVAC system, roof, plumbing, electrical system, and major appliances like the water heater, washer, dryer, refrigerator, and oven should all be assessed.

The property's location can also impact maintenance needs. For example, a beachfront property may require more frequent maintenance due to salt and moisture in the air, while a property in a colder climate may require winterization steps to prevent pipes from freezing.

Regular, ongoing maintenance tasks such as landscaping, cleaning, and pest control should also be factored in. Depending on the size of the property and your personal availability, you may need to hire professionals to manage these tasks.

Finally, consider the implications of maintenance on guest experience and property availability. Major maintenance or repair work may require the property to be vacant, which can lead to loss of rental income. Having a plan in place to address maintenance issues promptly and efficiently can minimize disruption to guests and downtime for the property.

ENERGY EFFICIENCY CONSIDERATIONS

Energy efficiency not only has direct implications for the operational costs of the property, but it is also an increasingly important factor for eco-conscious travelers. Inspect the property's insulation and windows. Good insulation helps keep the property warm in the winter and cool in the summer, reducing the need for heating and air conditioning. Similarly, double-glazed or energy-efficient windows can significantly reduce heat loss or gain, contributing to a more stable indoor temperature and lower energy bills.

Appliances and HVAC systems also play a significant role in a property's overall energy efficiency. When purchasing a property, look for modern, energy-efficient appliances and heating and cooling systems. These not only use less energy, but they may also last longer and perform better, enhancing your guests' comfort and experience. Remember to consider the age and efficiency of the water heater as well, as it is a significant contributor to energy usage.

Weigh the potential for renewable energy sources, like solar panels. While there's an upfront cost associated with installing solar panels, they can significantly reduce energy bills over time and even generate income if you're able to sell excess energy back to the grid.

Additionally, the property's lighting is another element to consider. Energy-efficient LED bulbs consume significantly less energy than traditional incandescent bulbs and also have a longer lifespan, reducing the need for replacements. Installing motion sensors in less-used areas can also help to minimize unnecessary energy use.

Water usage is another aspect of energy efficiency, particularly in areas prone to drought or with high water costs. Efficient plumbing fixtures like low-flow showerheads and dual-flush toilets can substantially reduce water usage.

Lastly, consider the property's landscaping and orientation. Shading elements, like trees or awnings, can reduce the need for air conditioning in the summer. The orientation of the property can also impact its natural light and heat and take advantage of natural sunlight to reduce the need for artificial lighting and heating.

By evaluating all these factors, you can lower operational costs, appeal to eco-conscious travelers, and contribute to a more sustainable tourism industry. Remember, the "perfect" vacation home will vary greatly depending on personal preferences and lifestyle needs. Therefore, it is essential to identify the features most important to you in your quest for the ideal vacation home that will also provide your potential renters with the attributes that will keep your property at the occupancy levels that you are looking for.

CHAPTER 7

REGULATORY, LEGAL, AND INSURANCE CONSIDERATIONS

The regulatory and legal landscape for short-term vacation rentals is continually evolving, so make sure you keep up-to-date with proposed and enacted laws that can have an impact on your vacation property. In some cases, municipalities are banning the use of a home for short-term rentals due to the impact that some are having on neighborhoods. In addition, this asset class has been under fire from the hotel industry as the competition has continued to impact occupancy rates in oversaturated markets.

When seeking a vacation home, it is critical to do the research and due diligence necessary to provide assurances that you are abiding by the local regulatory provisions. If a community where you want to rent a home out is not short-term rental friendly, you may as well immediately eliminate this location from consideration.

LOCAL ZONING AND REGULATIONS

Understanding legal and regulatory considerations when investing in a short-term vacation rental property is of utmost importance. Regulations governing vacation rentals can significantly impact the operation, profitability, and overall feasibility of your investment. By understanding the local laws, you can avoid the frustration of buying a vacation home, just to later learn that you are unable to use it as a short-term vacation rental.

As you begin your search for your perfect vacation home, you will immediately realize that different regions have varied regulations for short-term rentals. Some cities or counties may allow them freely, others may require specific licenses or permits, and some may prohibit them altogether. Ignorance of these regulations could result in fines, legal action, or the inability to rent your property. Therefore, researching local zoning laws, licensing requirements, and any restrictions on short-term rentals is a critical first step.

One of the countries my private equity fund invests in is Costa Rica, a beautiful vacation destination with laws and regulations that are very pro-tourism. Because tourism is the number-one industry in Costa Rica, the country welcomes the opportunity for people to invest in real estate and enhance the vacationer experience. Seek out communities like this that value and thrive on tourism.

TAXATION

Tax considerations can have a significant impact on your rental income, operating expenses, and overall profitability. Rental income from your vacation property is typically taxable. Depending on the number of days you rent out the property and the number of days you use it for personal use, different tax rules may apply. If you rent it out for more than fourteen days per year, you'll have to report all rental income to the IRS (or the relevant tax authority in your country). However, you'll also be able to deduct rental expenses, potentially reducing your tax liability.

Deductible rental expenses can include a wide range of costs, from mortgage interest and property taxes to maintenance, utilities, insurance, and depreciation. Understanding which expenses are deductible and how to accurately track and report them is key to minimizing your tax liability.

Another aspect to consider is local taxes. Many cities and municipalities impose an occupancy or tourist tax on short-term rentals. As the property owner, you may be responsible for collecting this tax from your guests and remitting it to the local government. Not complying with these requirements can lead to penalties and fines.

If you're considering purchasing a property in another state or country, you'll need to understand the specific tax laws and obligations in that location. This can include income taxes, sales taxes, property taxes, and potentially other levies. In some cases, double taxation treaties may exist to prevent you from being taxed twice on the same income.

Because tax laws are not consistent across countries, states, and municipalities, consider consulting with a tax advisor or real estate attorney who specializes in vacation rentals to ensure that you're fully informed and prepared for these tax considerations.

HOMEOWNER ASSOCIATIONS (HOA)

HOA rules can also significantly impact how you manage and operate your investment. HOAs exist in many residential communities and condominiums to maintain the quality and value of properties within their jurisdiction. They do this by setting and enforcing rules, known as covenants, conditions, and restrictions (CC&Rs). If the vacation property you're considering is part of an HOA, understanding these rules is crucial.

One of the first things to consider is whether the HOA permits short-term rentals at all. Some HOAs prohibit them entirely, while others may restrict the minimum rental period or limit the number of days per year a property can be rented. Ignoring these rules can lead to fines or legal action.

Even if short-term rentals are allowed, there may be other HOA rules that impact your rental property. For instance, there may be rules about noise levels, parking, garbage disposal, and use of common areas that could affect your guests. There may also be restrictions on property modifications or requirements for property maintenance that could impact your costs and flexibility.

It is also important to take into consideration the HOA's track record in conflict resolution. A cooperative and effective HOA can be a valuable partner in resolving any issues that may arise, while a contentious or unresponsive HOA could cause headaches.

By ensuring that your intended use of the property aligns with these rules and by considering the financial and operational implications of the HOA, you can avoid unexpected challenges and maximize the potential of your investment.

HOMEOWNER INSURANCE

Insurance provides a crucial financial safety net, protecting you from a multitude of risks ranging from property damage to legal liability. However, the insurance needs of a short-term rental property are often more complex than those of a typical home. When seeking out insurance options, find an insurance professional who is familiar with short-term rental properties to ensure you have the right coverage for your specific situation.

Standard homeowners' insurance might not provide adequate coverage for properties used as short-term rentals as these policies are typically designed for owner-occupied properties and may have exclusions or limitations for business activities, which can include short-term rentals. If a claim arises from an incident during a short-term rental, a standard homeowners' policy may not cover it.

Instead, you may need a specialized short-term rental insurance policy. These policies typically cover the same types of perils as a standard homeowners' policy, such as fire, theft, and liability, but without exclusions for short-term rental activities. They may also cover additional risks specific to rentals, such as loss of rental income if your property becomes uninhabitable due to a covered loss.

It is also worth noting that if you're renting your property through a platform like Airbnb or VRBO, they may offer some form of coverage. However, this coverage may not be comprehensive and is typically meant to supplement, not replace, your own insurance.

In some regions, insurance requirements may be dictated by local regulations or by the terms of your mortgage or homeowners' association. Be sure to investigate these requirements to ensure you're in compliance.

LIABILITY PROTECTION

Liability insurance provides critical protection against potential legal claims arising from incidents on your property. For example, if a guest slips on a loose stair and is injured, or if a faulty plumbing issue causes water damage to a guest's laptop, liability insurance would cover the associated costs, which could include medical expenses, repair or replacement costs, and even legal fees if the guest decides to sue.

Most standard homeowners' insurance policies include some degree of liability coverage, but there may be exclusions or limitations when the property is used for commercial purposes, such as short-term rentals. Therefore, securing a specific short-term rental insurance policy is often the best way to ensure you have adequate liability coverage.

These specialized policies are designed with the unique risks of short-term rentals in mind and typically provide more comprehensive liability coverage that applies even when you're renting out your property. Some policies may also cover additional liabilities unique to short-term rentals, such as those arising from services you provide to guests, such as bicycle or kayak rentals.

It's also worth noting that some short-term rental platforms offer a form of liability protection; however, these protections are often secondary to your own insurance and may not cover all potential liabilities. They also often have strict requirements for making a claim, and there may be certain exclusions. It's important to review these protections closely and consider them as a supplement to, not a replacement for, your own insurance.

When determining how much liability coverage you need, consider the value of your property, your personal financial assets, and the potential risks associated with your property. A higher level of coverage will typically come with a higher premium, but it can provide valuable peace of mind and financial protection.

BUSINESS INTERRUPTION INSURANCE

Business interruption insurance, also known as business income insurance, is a type of coverage that can play a vital role in protecting your short-term vacation rental business. While it is not typically a standalone product, it is often included or available as an add-on in certain commercial property insurance policies or specialized short-term rental insurance policies.

This type of insurance covers the loss of income that a business suffers after a disaster or significant disruption. In the context of a vacation rental, if a covered event like a fire, storm, or other types of physical damage makes your property uninhabitable for a period of time, business interruption insurance would cover the rental income you lose while the property is being repaired or rebuilt. This can be crucial for maintaining cash flow and meeting financial obligations like mortgage payments.

Business interruption insurance typically covers the revenue you would have earned, based on your financial records, had the disaster not occurred. The policy also covers operating expenses, like electricity, that continue even though business activities have come to a temporary halt.

It's important to note, however, that business interruption insurance usually only kicks in if the interruption is caused by a covered peril—that is, a type of damage or event that your policy specifically covers. Policies will typically not cover interruptions caused by perils that aren't included in your policy, so it's crucial to understand what is and isn't covered.

Moreover, business interruption insurance usually does not cover losses due to pandemics or communicable diseases. In the wake of the COVID-19 pandemic, many property owners discovered that their business interruption insurance did not cover their losses when they had to close or limit their rentals due to public health restrictions. Some insurance companies offer specialized coverage for these types of events, but they are usually separate from standard business interruption insurance.

GUEST PROPERTY INSURANCE

While guests are expected to take care of their personal belongings during their stay, there can be circumstances where their property gets damaged or lost. In these situations, guest property insurance comes into play.

Guest property insurance provides coverage for damage to or loss of a guest's personal property while they are staying at your vacation rental. For instance, if a fire or a plumbing leak in your rental property damages your guest's belongings, guest property insurance would cover the cost of replacing those items.

It's important to note that standard homeowner's or landlord insurance policies may not cover guest property. This is because those policies are typically designed to cover the property owner's belongings, not those of guests or tenants. To ensure coverage for guest property, you may need to look for a specialized short-term rental insurance policy or a specific endorsement to your existing policy.

Some vacation rental platforms offer a level of protection for guest property as part of their host guarantee or similar program. These protections can provide some coverage for guest belongings, but they typically come with restrictions, exclusions, and caps on payouts. They're also generally secondary to any other insurance you have, meaning they only pay out if your own insurance doesn't cover the loss.

While offering guest property insurance can provide peace of mind for your guests and potentially reduce your liability, it is still a good idea to encourage your guests to secure their own travel insurance. This type of insurance can cover not only their belongings but also trip cancellations, medical emergencies, and other travel-related risks.

RENTAL AGREEMENTS

When renting out a vacation property, you need to have a comprehensive rental agreement in place to protect your interests and outline the terms and conditions of the rental. Here are some key elements to include in a vacation property rental agreement:

Property Information

Begin the agreement by clearly identifying the vacation property being rented, including its address and any specific details that are relevant to the rental.

Rental Dates and Duration

Specify the rental period, including the check-in and check-out dates and times. Clearly define the duration of the rental, whether it's for a specific number of nights, weeks, or months.

Rental Fees and Payment Terms

Clearly state the rental fees, including the total amount due, any security deposit required, and the payment schedule. Outline the accepted forms of payment and any applicable late fees or penalties for non-payment.

Guest Responsibilities

Clearly define the responsibilities of the guest during their stay. This may include rules and guidelines for occupancy limits, noise restrictions, pet policies, smoking policies, and any other specific rules you have for the property.

Reservation and Cancellation Policies

Detail the reservation process, including any deposit or booking fees required to secure the reservation. Outline the cancellation policy, including any penalties or refunds based on the timing of the cancellation.

Maintenance and Repairs

Specify the guest's responsibilities regarding the maintenance and cleanliness of the property during their stay. Clarify your own responsibilities as the property owner to address any necessary repairs or maintenance during the rental period.

Liability and Insurance

Include a clause stating that the guest assumes liability for any damage or loss to the property during their stay. Specify that the property owner is not responsible for any accidents, injuries, or losses incurred by the guest or their invitees. You may also want to require guests to provide proof of their own travel insurance.

Dispute Resolution

Include a section outlining the procedure for resolving any disputes or disagreements that may arise between the parties, such as mediation or arbitration.

Governing Law

Specify the jurisdiction and governing law that applies to the rental agreement.

Signature and Date

Include spaces for both the property owner and the guest to sign and date the rental agreement, indicating their acceptance and understanding of the terms and conditions.

It is important to note that rental agreements can be subject to local laws and regulations, so it's advisable to consult with a legal professional familiar with vacation rental laws in your area to ensure compliance with all applicable rules and regulations.

TENANT SCREENING

Screening tenants for short-term vacation properties involves assessing their suitability and reliability as guests. Here are some steps you can take to screen potential tenants effectively:

Establish Rental Criteria

Determine the specific criteria you require in a guest, such as minimum age, maximum occupancy, and any specific rules or restrictions (e.g., no pets, no smoking). This will help you filter out unsuitable applicants.

Collect Guest Information

Create an application form or request essential information from potential guests. This may include their full name, contact information, purpose of visit, number of guests, and any special requirements or requests.

Conduct Background Checks

Consider conducting background checks to verify the credibility of potential guests. This may involve checking their references, reviewing their previous rental history, or searching for reviews or ratings if they have rented from other hosts or platforms in the past.

Communicate Clearly

Engage in clear and open communication with potential guests. Promptly respond to their inquiries and ask clarifying questions to assess their needs and intentions. Clear communication can help gauge their reliability and responsibility as guests.

Review Guest Profiles and Ratings

If you are using a vacation rental platform, review the guest's profile and any ratings or reviews they have received from previous hosts. This can provide valuable insights into their behavior and reliability.

Utilize Booking Platforms

Utilizing reputable vacation rental booking platforms can offer additional layers of protection and screening. These platforms often have guest verification processes and secure payment systems that can mitigate potential risks.

Request Identification

Ask potential guests to provide a copy of their identification, such as a driver's license or passport, to confirm their identity and ensure they meet your rental criteria.

Security Deposits

Consider requiring a security deposit to cover any potential damages or violations of rental terms. This helps incentivize guests to treat the property with care and provides a means for compensation if issues arise.

Trust Your Instincts

Trust your instincts and intuition during the screening process. If something feels off or you have reservations about a potential guest, it may be best to decline their reservation and continue searching for a more suitable tenant.

Have a Clear Rental Agreement

Implement a comprehensive rental agreement, as discussed in the previous response, that clearly outlines the terms and conditions of the rental. This provides a framework for both parties and sets expectations from the beginning.

Remember to comply with applicable laws and regulations related to tenant screening and privacy, ensuring that your screening process aligns with legal requirements and respects guests' rights.

CHAPTER 8

FINANCING YOUR INVESTMENT

When financing vacation home properties, you may find that the specific options available to you can depend on factors such as your financial situation, creditworthiness, the property itself, and the lender's requirements. And as we spoke about in earlier chapters, putting the right financing in place with the right lender terms can really boost the returns to your investment.

On the flip side, putting financing in place with terms that are not advantageous can also have a negative impact on your investment returns. This is why it is so critical to have a firm understanding of the financing vehicle that you want to put in place for your vacation home.

FINANCING OPTIONS AND MORTGAGE CONSIDERATIONS

There are many different financial vehicles available to consider when buying your short-term vacation rental. In this section, we will focus on the following financing options:

- Conventional Mortgages
- Second Mortgages
- Home Equity Lines of Credit (HELOCs) or Home Equity Loans
- Investment Property Loans
- Portfolio Loans
- Hard Money Loans
- Seller Financing
- Crowdfunding and Real Estate Investment Platforms

Conventional Mortgage

A conventional mortgage is a type of loan not guaranteed or insured by the federal government. These mortgages are popular choices for all kinds of home purchases, including short-term vacation rentals. If you're considering a conventional mortgage for your vacation rental property, there are a few key points to keep in mind.

Conventional mortgages are provided by private lenders like banks, credit unions, and online lenders. They typically require a down payment, which can be as low as 3% for a primary residence, but for an investment property like a vacation rental, the down payment requirement is usually higher, typically 20-30%. The exact amount can vary based on your credit score, the loan-to-value ratio, and other factors.

Interest rates for conventional mortgages are often competitive, especially for borrowers with strong credit. However, rates for investment properties can be higher than for primary residences. The exact rate will depend on your personal financial situation and market conditions.

Keep in mind that conventional mortgages for vacation rentals typically have stricter requirements for borrower credit scores, debt-to-income ratios, and cash reserves compared to primary residence loans. This is because lenders generally consider vacation rentals to be riskier investments.

Another thing to consider is the occupancy requirement. For a conventional mortgage on a second home, lenders typically require that the borrower uses the home for part of the year. If the property is rented out year-round, it is usually classified as an investment property, which may lead to higher interest rates and stricter underwriting standards.

You should also consider the impact of rental income on your loan approval. If you plan to rent out your vacation home, you might be able to use projected rental income to qualify for the mortgage. However, lenders often have specific guidelines for this. Some may require a history of rental income for the property, while others may only count a portion of the projected income.

A conventional mortgage can be a suitable choice for financing a vacation rental, but it's important to understand the unique requirements and considerations for this type of loan.

Second Home Mortgage

A second mortgage can be an appealing option when looking to finance a short-term vacation rental property. As the name suggests, a second mortgage is an additional loan taken out on a property that already has a mortgage. It is subordinate to the first mortgage, meaning it's paid off only after the first mortgage is fully repaid in case of default. When it comes to short-term vacation rentals, a few key points are worth considering regarding second mortgages.

Second mortgages typically have higher interest rates than first mortgages because they carry more risk for the lender. If you default on your loans, your first mortgage will be repaid before any funds go towards the second mortgage. Despite the higher interest rates, a second mortgage can still be a cost-effective way to finance a vacation rental property, particularly if it helps you avoid mortgage insurance on the rental property loan.

However, it is crucial to understand that when you take out a second mortgage, you're putting your primary residence at risk. If you're unable to keep up with the payments on the second mortgage, the lender could foreclose on your home. Therefore, you must be confident in your ability to manage the additional debt, as well as the costs and potential income fluctuations associated with a short-term vacation rental.

In addition, lenders typically have strict requirements for second mortgages, including a good credit score, low debt-to-income ratio, and significant equity in your primary residence. They may also require proof of income that will support both your first and second mortgage payments.

Home Equity Line of Credit (HELOC)

A Home Equity Line of Credit, or HELOC, can be a flexible financing tool when purchasing a short-term vacation rental property. A HELOC allows you to tap into the equity of your existing property and use it as a line of credit, much like a credit card. You only pay interest on the funds you use, and you can reuse the credit line as you pay it off.

A HELOC can provide the necessary funds for a down payment on a vacation rental property or even fund the entire purchase, depending on how much equity you have in your current property. This can be particularly useful if you want to secure a property quickly, as you can draw on the line of credit as soon as it's established, which can often be faster than securing a new mortgage.

Interest rates for HELOCs are typically variable, which means they can increase or decrease over the life of the line of credit. These rates are often lower than credit card interest rates, but can be higher than mortgage rates. It's also important to note that the interest you pay on a HELOC used to buy a vacation rental could be tax-deductible as a business expense.

Because the interest rate on this type of loan is variable, it is important to consider the ramifications of increasing interest rates. For example, due to the decision by the Federal Reserve to significantly raise the federal funds rate, mortgage rates nearly doubled from late 2022 into early 2023. This had a negative impact on investors who had HELOCs in place. Always have a clear understanding of the impacts interest rates have on your profitability.

Using a HELOC also comes with other risks. Because a HELOC is secured by your home, failure to repay can result in the loss of that home. Additionally, because the interest rate is variable, your payments can increase if interest rates rise. Some HELOCs also have balloon payments at the end of the term, which could require you to pay off the entire balance at once or refinance the debt.

When considering a HELOC for a short-term vacation rental, remember that the rental income from the property may be variable. While vacation rentals can generate significant income during high-demand periods, there may be times when the property is unoccupied. It's important to ensure that you can afford the HELOC payments, even if your rental income is lower than expected.

Investment Property Loans

Investment property loans are a form of financing specifically designed for individuals or businesses that want to buy a property for the purpose of earning a return on the investment through rental income, the future resale of the property, or both. These loans can be an excellent fit for those looking to invest in short-term vacation rentals.

Investment property loans differ from primary residence mortgages in several ways. First, they typically come with higher interest rates. The rate is usually 0.5% to 0.75% higher than what you'd see on a primary residence loan because lenders perceive investment properties as having a higher risk compared to primary residences due to borrowers being more likely to default on an investment property loan than a primary residence loan.

Down payment requirements are also usually higher for investment property loans. While you might be able to put down as little as 3% to 5% on a primary residence, expect to put down at least 20% to 25% for an investment property loan. Some lenders may even require a larger down payment for properties intended as short-term vacation rentals.

Lenders also look closely at potential rental income when considering an investment property loan application. Some may require you to demonstrate that the potential rental income will cover at least one-and-a-quarter times your mortgage payment. This is an especially important factor for short-term rentals since they can have more variable income than long-term rentals due to seasonal demand and other factors.

Qualifying for an investment property loan often requires a good to excellent credit score, a low debt-to-income ratio, and adequate cash reserves. Lenders may want to see that you have enough cash on hand to cover several months of mortgage payments, particularly for a short-term vacation rental property where rental income may be less predictable.

Portfolio Loans

Unlike conventional loans, which are sold to investors on the secondary market, portfolio loans are kept "in-house" by the lending institution that originates them. This can offer greater flexibility and open up opportunities for borrowers who may not fit the standard lending criteria.

Portfolio loans can be particularly useful for real estate investors who already have multiple properties. Conventional lenders may limit the number of mortgages a single borrower can have, but because portfolio lenders set their own rules, they may be willing to finance additional properties. This can make a portfolio loan an attractive option if you're looking to expand your portfolio of short-term vacation rentals.

Another advantage of portfolio loans is their flexibility. Portfolio lenders can set their own underwriting criteria, which means they may be more willing to consider alternative documentation of income or assets, or to work with borrowers who have unique situations. For example, if you expect your vacation rental to generate significant income, but you don't have a long history of rental earnings, a portfolio lender might be more willing to take that projected income into account.

Portfolio loans can also provide flexibility in terms of the property itself. If you're considering a vacation rental that is unique or unconventional in some way, a portfolio lender might be more open to financing it than a conventional lender would be.

However, portfolio loans typically come with higher interest rates than conventional mortgages, and they may also have higher origination fees or other costs. The exact terms will vary by lender and depend on factors like your credit score, the size of your down payment, and the specifics of the property.

Hard Money Loans

Hard money loans can be a useful tool in certain situations when looking to finance a short-term vacation rental property. These loans are typically issued by private investors or companies, rather than banks or credit unions, and have different advantages and drawbacks than traditional financing methods.

One of the key features of hard money loans is that they are asset-based. This means the lender focuses more on the value of the property you're investing in, rather than your credit history or income. If you have less-than-stellar credit or a non-traditional income source, a hard money loan could potentially still be an option for you.

Hard money loans are also typically processed much faster than conventional loans. This speed can be a significant advantage in competitive real estate markets where being able to move quickly can mean the difference between securing a desirable property and losing out to another buyer. If you find a vacation rental property that you believe is a great investment opportunity, a hard money loan could help you secure the property quickly.

However, hard money loans come with a number of drawbacks. They are usually short-term loans, often with terms of only a few years or even less. This means you'll need to either sell the property or refinance into a more traditional loan fairly quickly.

Moreover, the interest rates on hard money loans are typically much higher than those of traditional loans, and hefty origination fees are common. While these costs might be feasible if you're expecting to turn around and sell the property quickly at a profit or if you anticipate significant rental income, they can add up if your plans take longer to realize than you initially anticipated.

If you're considering a hard money loan for a short-term vacation rental, it's critical to have a clear plan for how you'll pay off the loan, whether through selling the property, refinancing, or rental income.

Seller Financing

With seller financing, the property's current owner agrees to finance all or part of the purchase price, essentially acting as the bank. The buyer then makes payments to the seller over time, as they would with a mortgage. This arrangement can have several benefits but also comes with potential drawbacks.

One of the main advantages of seller financing is flexibility. The terms of the financing, such as the down payment, interest rate, and repayment schedule, are negotiable between the buyer and seller. This can make it a good option for buyers who may not qualify for traditional financing or who are seeking specific terms that a bank can't provide. For instance, the seller might agree to a lower down payment or a longer repayment term than a bank would offer.

Another benefit is speed. Because you're not waiting for a bank's approval, the closing process can often be completed more quickly with seller financing. This can be advantageous in a competitive market or when the seller is eager to close the deal.

However, seller financing also has potential downsides. The interest rate may be higher than what you'd pay with a traditional mortgage. And because the seller is not a regulated financial institution, they don't have to offer you the same borrower protections that a bank would. There's also the risk that if the seller still has a mortgage on the property and doesn't make their payments, the bank could foreclose, leaving you without the property and without the money you've paid toward it.

As with any financing option, it's critical to thoroughly understand the terms of the agreement and ideally to seek advice from a real estate attorney or financial advisor. It's also wise to have the property and the seller's financial situation thoroughly vetted to ensure there are no hidden issues.

Crowdfunding and Real Estate Investment Platforms

Crowdfunding and real estate investment platforms allow investors to pool their money together to invest in properties, often without the need to manage the properties themselves. This presents an opportunity for individuals to participate in the real estate market who may not have the resources to purchase a property outright.

Crowdfunding is particularly attractive because it can provide access to a variety of property types, locations, and investment structures. For example, an individual could invest in a share of a luxury vacation rental property in a popular destination that would be otherwise unattainable for most individual investors.

Real estate investment platforms, such as Real Estate Investment Trusts (REITs) or online platforms like Fundrise or RealtyMogul, offer similar opportunities. These platforms allow investors to purchase shares in a portfolio of properties, which can provide diversification and potential steady returns from rental income and appreciation.

For example, my company, Blue Fusion Capital, manages private equity funds that invest in short-term vacation rentals throughout the world. We have both accredited and non-accredited funds that allow investors to invest as little as $2,000 into short-term vacation rental investments. If you would like to learn more about our investment opportunities, you can visit our website at bluefusioncapital.com.

One of the significant advantages of these methods is the potential for passive income. Unlike owning a property directly, investors in crowdfunding projects or through investment platforms generally don't need to worry about finding tenants, maintaining properties, or dealing with other day-to-day aspects of property management.

However, as with any investment, there are risks involved. The success of your investment is largely out of your control and depends on the performance of the property or portfolio of properties. There's also less liquidity in these investments compared to stocks or bonds, meaning it can be difficult to sell your shares quickly if you need to cash out.

Furthermore, while these platforms can open up opportunities to invest in vacation rentals, they often don't offer the same level of control or potential profitability as buying a property outright. There can also be fees associated with these platforms, so it's crucial to understand the fee structure before investing.

Crowdfunding and real estate investment platforms can provide an avenue for investing in short-term vacation rentals, especially for those who prefer a more hands-off approach. But as with any investment, understanding the potential rewards and risks is vital.

Consult with multiple lenders, compare loan terms, interest rates, and closing costs, and thoroughly evaluate the financial implications of each option. A mortgage broker or financial advisor can provide guidance tailored to your specific situation and help you navigate the various financial options available for vacation home properties.

FINANCING CASE STUDY—IMPACT OF FINANCING ON ROI

In the Valuation Analysis chapter of this book, we introduced the fundamentals behind leveraging financing to decrease the amount of cash you are required to put into your vacation home investment and increase your return on investment. The capitalization rate is the return on your investment if you execute your purchase using 100% cash and no financing leverage.

Leveraging your property can increase your returns, but it is important to make sure the interest rate you are paying is adequate to increase your returns. To illustrate this, we will do a case study using the properties we presented in the Valuation Analysis chapter of this book.

Costa Rica Home

For this financing case study, we will use the previous example based in Costa Rica. Here is a refresher on those details:

FOR SALE: $900,000

BEDROOMS:	4 Bedroom	**SQUARE FEET:**	4.200 SF
BATHROOMS:	4 Bathrooms	**LOT SIZE:**	12.390 SF
SLEEPS:	10 People	**FURNISHED:**	Fully

The property is located in Costa Rica, has excellent ocean views, and is a short 5-minute walk to the beach and town. The investor was provided with the prior year's historical expense data for the property; however, the home has not historically been operated as a short-term vacation rental, so there is no historical revenue information available.

Example ProForma Operating Statement

As was demonstrated earlier in the book, the estimated capitalization rate for this property was projected at 10.82%. We now want to introduce financing vehicles to demonstrate the impact of financing on your rate of return.

	PROFORMA	
	AVERAGE DAILY RATE (ADR)	$550
(x)	DAYS AVAILABLE FOR RENT	365
(=)	POTENTIAL GROSS INCOME	$200,750
(x)	OCCUPANCY (%)	70%
(=)	EFFECTIVE GROSS INCOME	$140,525
(-)	LESS PROJECTED EXPENSES	
	REAL ESTATE TAXES	$4,120
	INSURANCE	$2,000
	HOA DUES	$3,000
	GAS/ELECTRIC	$3,605
	TRASH	$0
	INTERNET/TV	$0
	REPAIRS AND MAINTENANCE	$3,000
	ADMINISTRATION (1.5% EGI)	$2,108
	PROPERTY LISTING SERVICES (3% EGI)	$4,216
	MANAGEMENT FEES (15% EGI)	$21,079
(=)	PROJECTED NOI	$97,397
(/)	DIVIDED BY PURCHASE PRICE	$900,000
(=)	ESTIMATED CAP RATE	10.82%

Introducing Financing

Let's take the Net Operating Income from the previous ProForma and place debt service on the property to demonstrate what the impact is on your project Return on Investment. The formula for calculating the net cashflow is

- **Net Operating Income (NOI) (-) Annual Interest Expense (=) Net Cashflow.**

Next, the formula for calculating the ROI based on introducing financing is:

- **Net Cashflow (/) Cash Amount (=) Annual Rate of Return.**

INTRODUCING FINANCING

ASSUMPTIONS

Capitalization Rate at 100% Cash	= 10.82%
Loan Amount at 70% LTV	= $630,000
Cash Amount at 30% LTV	= $270,000

7% INTEREST

Net Operating Income	= $97,397	
Interest Only Expense @ 7%	= $44,100	**19.74%**
Net Cashflow	= $53,297	
Cash Amount	= $270,000	

8% INTEREST

Net Operating Income	= $97,397	
Interest Only Expense @ 8%	= $50,400	**17.41%**
Net Cashflow	= $46,997	
Cash Amount	= $270,000	

9% INTEREST

Net Operating Income	= $97,397	
Interest Only Expense @ 9%	= $56,700	**15.07%**
Net Cashflow	= $40,697	
Cash Amount	= $270,000	

As you can see above, we used the Net Operating Income of $97,000 from our example property. We then estimated the Interest Only Expense based on the projected interest rate. As an example, if the loan amount is $630,000 and the interest rate is 7%, the Interest Only Expense would be **$44,100** ($630,000 Loan Amount x 7% Interest Rate = Interest Only Expense).

Interest Rate Impact

Now that we have calculated the annual rate of return once we have put financing in place, it is possible to see what impact the interest we have to pay on the loan will have on our returns.

The first thing to take note of is the impact that paying a loan has on your Net Operating Income to get to a Net Cashflow. We had to deduct the interest costs from the NOI to get to a Net Cashflow. When the interest costs go up, the Net Cashflow goes down, and when the Net Cashflow goes down, your Annual Rate of Return also goes down. This is why you need to pay particular attention to the interest rate you will be paying on the loan. The lower the interest rate, the higher the Annual Rate of Return.

In the example above, the Cap Rate was estimated at a 10.82% return on cash, so even getting a loan at 9% would increase your Annual Rate of Return to 15.07% and would be worth putting in place. However, you should be very aware of how these calculations have an impact on one another. If the cost is too high, it can push the Annual Rate of Return below the Capitalization Rate. In these cases, it would not be financially prudent to put the expensive debt on the property.

Financing can be an important component when you are looking for ways to increase the rate of return on your vacation home investment. However, it is important to have a clear understanding of the impacts that the interest rate and loan costs can have on your returns.

To streamline these calculations, download our FREE valuation tool spreadsheet at vacationpropertysecrets.com/freevaluationtool. This spreadsheet is fully automated and will have you making these calculations with ease.

CHAPTER 9

PROPERTY ACQUISITION

Y ou have done the due diligence and research that has led up to this very moment—it is time to purchase your vacation home property! There is *nothing* like the feeling of getting a high-potential vacation property under contract.

And you're almost there! At this point, it is all about working through the purchasing process and the negotiations necessary to get the best deal, and then pushing for pricing that will give you the best returns on your investment.

WORKING WITH REAL ESTATE AGENTS AND BROKERS

Finding the right real estate agent or broker is crucial, and engaging a broker who understands the fundamentals of the short-term vacation rental market is very important. They not only facilitate the property search and buying process but also provide invaluable advice and insights based on their experience and knowledge of the market.

You should consider their expertise in the vacation rental market. This is a specialized segment of the real estate market with unique considerations, such as zoning regulations, licensing requirements, and short-term rental market dynamics. An agent or broker with experience in this field will be better equipped to advise you on these matters and help you avoid potential pitfalls.

Next, assess their local knowledge. Real estate is inherently local; the profitability of a short-term rental can be heavily influenced by factors like the property's location, local demand for vacation rentals, and competition. An agent or broker with deep knowledge of the local market can help you identify promising areas and accurately estimate potential rental income.

Look for an agent or broker who has a solid track record of successful transactions in the short-term rental market. They should be able to provide references from satisfied clients who have purchased similar properties. This track record not only indicates their competence but also their understanding of the unique needs and concerns of short-term rental investors.

Consider their level of professionalism and customer service. They should be responsive, transparent, and dedicated to serving your best interests. They should also be willing to take the time to understand your investment goals, answer your questions, and guide you through the process.

Be sure to take the time to research potential agents or brokers, interview them, and choose the one who is the best fit for your specific needs and goals.

AGENCY RELATIONSHIPS

In real estate transactions, agency relationships describe the legal relationship between the agent or broker and the parties involved in a transaction, typically the buyer and the seller. There are three main types of agency relationships: seller's agency, buyer's agency, and dual agency. Understanding these relationships is important as they define the legal responsibilities and obligations an agent or broker has towards their clients.

Seller's Agency

Also known as a listing agent, a seller's agent represents the interests of the seller. The agent's primary duties are to the seller, and they include marketing the property, negotiating the best possible price and terms, and guiding the seller through the selling process.

The seller's agent has a fiduciary duty to the seller, meaning they must act in the seller's best interest at all times. When listing your property, you want to make sure you have a seller's agency agreement in place with a professional who is looking out for your best interests.

Buyer's Agency

A buyer's agent represents the interests of the buyer in a real estate transaction. The agent assists the buyer in searching for a property, making an offer, negotiating terms, and navigating the buying process. Like a seller's agent, a buyer's agent has a fiduciary duty to the buyer and must act in the buyer's best interest. When buying your vacation home, you want the agency agreement to be very clear about who is representing whom.

When making a vacation home purchase, make certain that you can put a buyer's agency agreement in place so the professional you engage is working on behalf of *you* and *your* best interests. This allows you to have confidential conversations about the investment and offer strategies with the broker/salesperson without the information being passed on to the other side of the deal.

Dual Agency

In some cases, an agent or broker may represent both the buyer and the seller in the same transaction. This is known as dual agency. In this situation, the agent has a fiduciary duty to both parties. Dual agency can be challenging because the agent must balance the interests of both the buyer and the seller, and it can potentially lead to conflicts of interest.

In some states, dual agency is not allowed, and in others, it requires the informed consent of both parties. There is also a "transaction broker" or "facilitator" relationship where the agent doesn't represent either party but facilitates the transaction. This role is more neutral, and the agent doesn't owe a fiduciary duty to either party.

Anyone involved in a real estate transaction needs to understand these agency relationships and the obligations that come with them. Clients should also confirm the type of relationship in writing with their agent to avoid any potential misunderstandings or conflicts of interest.

If you are searching for a reliable, trustworthy agent, I can help. I have compiled a network of real estate professionals throughout the world who understand the short-term vacation rental market and processes. If you would like for me to connect you with a professional who specializes in this property type, you can get more information at vacationpropertysecrets.com.

NEGOTIATING THE RIGHT PRICE

Negotiation is a crucial skill that can make the difference between a good deal and a missed opportunity. Employing the right strategies can potentially save you thousands of dollars and help you secure the property you desire. I personally love the negotiation process. It is a thrill to lock down an opportunity that will provide the best chances for success and the highest potential returns to the vacation home investment.

One of the most effective negotiation techniques in real estate is to do your homework. That means conducting thorough research on the property, the market, and the seller. Understanding the local real estate market conditions, the property's specifics, including its condition and unique features, as well as the seller's motivations, can give you valuable insight that you can use to your advantage. For example, if a seller needs to move quickly, they may be more willing to accept a lower price.

Always consider leading with a strong opening offer. The initial offer sets the stage for the negotiation, and a lowball offer might offend the seller, souring the relationship. However, offering too high might leave money on the table. The trick is to balance your interests with a realistic approach that respects the fair market value of the property. A competitive offer demonstrates your serious intent to purchase and can motivate the seller to engage more positively in the negotiation.

Recently, I was negotiating a property in Costa Rica where the listing price for the property was $999,000, and the property was being sold at an advantageous 15% capitalization rate. It was actually priced well at $999,000; however, a lower price would mean a better capitalization rate. The following shows what the Net Operating Income would be at a 15% capitalization rate:

- **($999,000 List Price x 15% Cap Rate) = $149,850 Net Operating Income**

But just because it has an attractive capitalization rate does not mean it couldn't be better! In this case, we made our initial offer at $850,000. This was nearly a 15% discount from the asking price. It was not a recent listing, but it had also not been on the market terribly long. In this case, the seller reiterated that we were dealing with a 15% capitalization rate, and they asked us to come back to the table with a number that we could begin negotiations with.

We then upped our offer to $900,000 (nearly a 10% discount), and the sellers came back to us with their lowest and best offer at $950,000. When negotiating, you always want to take the emotion out of the purchase; your goal should be to get the seller's lowest and best offer.

Now, when you take into consideration their lowest price, the capitalization rate is even more advantageous than 15%. That math looks like this:

- **($149,850 Net Operating Income / $950,000 Purchase Price) = 15.77% Cap Rate**

In this case we were able to increase our projected return by nearly three fourths of a basis point, and when it comes to an investment property, every dollar matters!

It is also important to be flexible and focus on the bigger picture. While price is important, other terms such as closing dates, contingencies, and repairs might be equally crucial for the seller. If you can provide flexibility where the seller needs it most, they might be willing to compromise on other points.

Negotiating with a pre-approval letter can also give you an advantage. As mentioned earlier, if you are not buying the home with cash, the letter from a lender shows that you have the financial capacity to purchase the property and can make your offer stand out, especially in a competitive market. A seller wants to know that you have the financial ability to get a deal to the finish line. There is nothing worse for a seller than to put a property under contract simply to have the deal fall apart because the buyer could not financially get it to the closing table. The stronger your financial position, the better your negotiation position.

Lastly, strategically using silence can be a powerful tool in negotiations. If you've made a fair offer or asked a critical question, wait for the seller to respond. Don't rush to fill the silence or change your offer; let them consider your proposal.

Remember, the goal of negotiation is to get to the seller's lowest and best price while reaching a win-win solution that satisfies both parties. Maintaining a respectful, professional demeanor throughout the process is essential to achieving this outcome.

PROPERTY INSPECTIONS

When buying a vacation home, it is essential to conduct a thorough property inspection to assess its condition and identify any potential issues. Here are some types of property inspections you should consider:

General Home Inspection

A general home inspection is a comprehensive examination of the property's overall condition. It covers the structure, interior, exterior, electrical systems, plumbing, HVAC (heating, ventilation, and air conditioning), roofing, insulation, and more. This inspection helps identify any visible defects, safety concerns, or maintenance issues.

Pest Inspection

A pest inspection, often conducted by a licensed pest control professional, examines the property for the presence of pests, such as termites, rodents, or insects. This inspection is particularly crucial in areas prone to specific pests, as they can cause significant damage to the property.

Environmental Assessment

Depending on the location and potential risks, you may want to consider additional assessments, such as radon testing, lead-based paint inspection (especially in older properties), or testing for mold or other indoor air quality concerns.

Septic System Inspection

If the vacation home has a septic system, it is advisable to have it inspected by a professional to ensure it is functioning properly and not in need of repairs or replacement.

Well Inspection

In properties with a private well for water supply, a well inspection is necessary to evaluate the quality and functionality of the well system.

Roof Inspection

Engaging a qualified roofing professional to inspect the roof can help identify any existing or potential issues, such as leaks, damaged shingles, or the need for repairs or replacement.

Electrical and Plumbing Inspections

Consider hiring licensed electricians and plumbers to assess the electrical and plumbing systems thoroughly. They can identify any code violations, safety concerns, or potential issues that may require attention.

It's important to hire qualified and reputable professionals to conduct these inspections. They will provide you with detailed reports, including any recommended repairs or further investigations needed. Based on the inspection results, you can make informed decisions about the property purchase, negotiate repairs with the seller, or budget for necessary repairs or upgrades.

Remember, the specific inspections required may vary depending on factors such as the property's age, location, and any specific concerns identified during the buying process.

DUE DILIGENCE

When buying a vacation home, conducting thorough due diligence is crucial to ensure a successful and informed purchase. Here are some key aspects to consider.

Property Inspection

As mentioned earlier, conduct a comprehensive property inspection to assess the condition of the vacation home and identify any potential issues or repairs needed. This helps you understand the property's overall quality and can influence your decision-making process.

Title Search and Ownership Verification

Hire a title company or real estate attorney to perform a title search and verify ownership of the property. This ensures that the seller has a clear and marketable title and there are no liens, encumbrances, or legal issues that could affect your ownership rights.

Review of Property Documents

Carefully review all relevant property documents, including the deed, survey reports, zoning restrictions, HOA rules and regulations (if applicable), and any existing leases or rental agreements. Pay attention to any restrictions or limitations that may affect your planned use or rental of the property.

Financial Analysis

Conduct a financial analysis to assess the costs and potential income associated with the vacation home. This includes evaluating property taxes, insurance premiums, utility expenses, maintenance costs, and any potential rental income or occupancy rates. It helps you determine the financial viability of the investment and whether it aligns with your goals.

Local Regulations and Zoning

Research local regulations, zoning ordinances, and any restrictions that may affect the property. This includes understanding short-term rental regulations, building codes, and any other local requirements that may impact your ability to use the property as desired.

Insurance Considerations

Investigate insurance options and costs specific to the vacation home. Obtain quotes for property insurance, liability insurance, flood insurance (if applicable), and any additional coverage you may require. And ensure that insurance is available at a reasonable cost and that it adequately covers your needs.

Rental Market Analysis

If you plan to rent out the vacation home, conduct a rental market analysis. Evaluate rental demand, occupancy rates, rental prices, and competition in the area. This analysis helps you understand the potential rental income and the viability of your investment as a rental property.

Professional Advice

Seek advice from professionals such as real estate agents, attorneys, accountants, and property managers who have experience in the vacation rental market. They can provide valuable insights, guidance, and help you make informed decisions.

Financing Options

If you require financing for the vacation home, explore different mortgage options and lenders, comparing interest rates, loan terms, and eligibility criteria to secure the best financing option for your specific situation.

Remember, due diligence requirements may vary based on factors such as the property's location, type, and your individual circumstances. It is advisable to work with qualified professionals who can guide you through the due diligence process and provide tailored advice based on your specific needs and the property you intend to purchase.

CLOSING THE DEAL

Closing day is an exciting time! You finally get to take ownership of your vacation home. There is nothing quite like walking away from the closing table with keys in hand! However, closing the deal on a vacation home requires careful attention to detail and coordination of various tasks.

Engage Professionals

Work with a real estate attorney or title company experienced in vacation home transactions. They will ensure all necessary legal documents and paperwork are in order, and the closing process is handled correctly.

Review Closing Documents

Carefully review all closing documents, including the purchase agreement, title commitment, loan documents (if applicable), and any other relevant paperwork. Understand the terms, conditions, and obligations outlined in these documents.

Conduct Final Walk-Through

Schedule a final walk-through of the property shortly before the closing to ensure it is in the agreed-upon condition and that any repairs or agreed-upon changes have been completed satisfactorily.

Complete Financing Arrangements

If you are obtaining financing for the vacation home, ensure all necessary documents are provided to your lender promptly. Coordinate with your lender to meet any loan requirements and secure final loan approval before the closing date.

Obtain Insurance

Arrange for property insurance coverage that takes effect on the closing date, and provide proof of insurance to the appropriate parties, such as the lender or title company.

Coordinate with the Title Company

Stay in close communication with the title company or closing agent handling the transaction. Provide any required information, sign documents in a timely manner, and address any questions or concerns they may have.

Review Closing Costs

Review the closing costs outlined in the closing statement (HUD-1 or Closing Disclosure), and make sure you understand each item. Address any discrepancies or questions with the closing agent.

Transfer Utilities and Services

Coordinate with utility companies to transfer or establish accounts in your name for electricity, water, gas, internet, and other services. Ensure services are scheduled to be activated or transferred on the closing date or shortly after.

Arrange for Funds

Determine the amount and method of payment for the closing costs and any required funds for the transaction. Coordinate with your financial institution to ensure the funds are available in the appropriate form (e.g., cashier's check or wire transfer) before the closing.

Attend the Closing

Plan to attend the closing appointment in person or virtually, as required. Bring any necessary identification and copies of important documents, such as your driver's license or passport.

Conduct a Thorough Review

Before signing any documents, carefully review each page and ensure they accurately reflect the terms and conditions agreed upon. Ask questions if anything is unclear.

Maintain Communication

Stay in contact with your real estate agent, attorney, or closing agent throughout the closing process. Address any last-minute issues promptly, and ensure all required steps are completed before the closing date.

By following these tips and staying organized, you can help ensure a smooth and successful closing on your vacation home.

CHAPTER 10

MARKETING AND MAXIMIZING RENTAL INCOME

At this point, you have done your due diligence and purchased your vacation home. It is now time to begin my favorite part of the process—taking the property to market. One of the most important parts of your success will be the proper marketing of the property and making certain you are maximizing the rental income you bring in.

When we bring a new property into our portfolio, we have a very good grasp of what the market is doing in terms of property performance, but we always look for ways that we can exceed expectations and outperform the market. We always want to be exceptional at what we are doing.

In this chapter, you will learn processes and techniques we use to get the best results for the vacation homes that we own. As you go through this journey, refer back to this chapter often to continually evolve as a vacation homeowner. The methods and insights contained in this chapter include:

- Defining your target market
- Establishing your unique selling points
- Utilizing the online platforms and listing sites
- Learning pricing strategies and how to optimize rental rates
- Creating a guest experience and excellent customer service
- How to use customer feedback
- Understanding best photography practices
- Using virtual tours
- Creating effective property listings
- Building a website that converts
- Offering a guidebook
- Getting to Superhost status
- Receiving 5-star reviews
- Providing last-minute bookings

DEVELOPING A MARKETING STRATEGY FOR YOUR VACATION RENTAL

Developing a marketing strategy for a short-term vacation rental is vital for the success of the investment. The vacation rental market is highly competitive, and with the growing popularity of platforms like Airbnb and VRBO, guests now have a vast array of options at their fingertips.

Without a sound marketing strategy, your property could easily be overlooked in favor of others with a more visible or appealing online presence. A well-crafted marketing strategy will highlight the unique selling points of your property, reach your target audience, and ultimately, increase your occupancy rates and return on investment.

Effective marketing can also build a strong reputation for your rental, leading to repeat bookings and word-of-mouth referrals, which are invaluable in the long term. Hence, marketing isn't merely an optional extra—it's an integral part of operating a successful short-term vacation rental.

DEFINE YOUR TARGET MARKET

A key component of a successful marketing strategy for a short-term vacation rental is understanding and defining your target market, which consists of the guests who are most likely to rent your property. The more you understand about them, their needs, preferences, and behaviors, the better you can tailor your marketing efforts to attract them.

Start by considering the location and characteristics of your property. If your vacation rental is located near a beach, your target market may consist of families looking for a beach vacation, or couples seeking a tranquil seaside retreat. If it's in a city center, your target guests may be business travelers or tourists interested in cultural and urban attractions. If your property is in a mountainous region with nearby ski resorts, then winter sports enthusiasts may be your ideal guests.

Consider the size and amenities of your property. A small, one-bedroom apartment would likely appeal to couples or solo travelers, while a larger home with multiple bedrooms and a backyard would be more suitable for families or groups. Amenities such as a fully equipped kitchen, fast Wi-Fi, a hot tub, or a home office setup can also influence who is likely to book your property.

Once you've identified who your potential guests are, dig a little deeper to understand their preferences and behaviors. What are they looking for in a vacation rental? What platforms do they use to search for and book properties? What price range are they comfortable with? This information can inform your listing description, pricing strategy, and the platforms you choose to list your property on.

Understanding the demographics of your target market is also crucial. Factors such as age, income level, occupation, and even lifestyle habits can greatly impact a person's travel and accommodation preferences. For instance, younger travelers might value trendy decor and proximity to nightlife, while older guests might prioritize comfort and tranquility.

By identifying and focusing on your target market, you can ensure that your marketing efforts are reaching the right people and ultimately increase your booking rates and profitability. Remember, your aim is not to appeal to everyone but to attract and satisfy those guests who are most suited to what your property has to offer.

ESTABLISH UNIQUE SELLING POINTS

Establishing the unique selling points (USPs) of your short-term vacation rental is an essential part of your marketing strategy. USPs are what set your property apart from the competition and make it attractive to potential guests. By focusing on your unique selling points, you can differentiate your property from the competition, attract your target market, and ultimately increase your booking rates and profitability.

To identify your property's USPs, start by considering its physical characteristics. What features does it have that other properties don't? This could be anything from a stunning view, a prime location, or unique architectural details, to high-quality furnishings, a well-equipped kitchen, or tech amenities such as high-speed Wi-Fi or smart home features.

Next, consider the broader context of your property. Is it located in a particularly desirable neighborhood, close to popular tourist attractions, or in a peaceful, secluded spot? Is there a popular cafe, a park, or a unique shop nearby? Location-based USPs can be a powerful draw for potential guests, especially those who value convenience or are looking for an authentic local experience.

And don't forget about the experience you offer to your guests. Exceptional customer service can be a powerful USP. This could be your responsiveness to inquiries, the ease of the check-in process, or the extra steps you take to ensure your guests have a comfortable and enjoyable stay. This might include a welcome basket with local goodies, personalized recommendations for local attractions, or simply being available and approachable should your guests have any questions or issues.

Once you've identified your USPs, it's crucial to communicate them effectively in your marketing materials. High-quality photos and detailed, engaging descriptions can help potential guests visualize the unique features and experiences that your property offers. Highlight your USPs in your property listing, on your website, and in your social media posts.

ONLINE PLATFORMS AND LISTING SITES

Online platforms and listing sites have become the primary means for guests to find and book short-term vacation rentals. Booking sites attract millions of users from around the world and can provide extensive exposure for your rental property.

Some of the most popular booking sites and platforms include

- **Airbnb:** Airbnb is one of the most popular vacation rental platforms worldwide. It has a large user base and offers a user-friendly interface for hosts to list their properties. Airbnb allows hosts to set their own prices, manage availability, and communicate with guests.

- **HomeAway/VRBO:** HomeAway and VRBO are part of the Expedia Group and are widely recognized platforms for vacation rentals. They provide a global reach and attract a diverse range of travelers. These platforms offer features such as calendar synchronization, secure payment processing, and direct communication with guests.

- **Booking.com:** Booking.com is a leading online travel agency that offers a wide range of accommodation options, including vacation rentals. It has a large user base and provides a platform for hosts to list their properties and manage bookings. Booking. com offers various tools and features to optimize your listing's performance.

- **TripAdvisor:** TripAdvisor is a popular travel platform that allows hosts to list their vacation rentals. It provides a large audience of travelers who use the platform to research and book accommodations. TripAdvisor offers tools for managing bookings, reviews, and communication with guests.

- **Expedia:** Expedia is another major online travel agency that offers vacation rental listings and provides tools for managing bookings, pricing, and availability. By listing your property on Expedia, you can reach a broad audience of travelers who use the platform to book accommodations.

- **FlipKey:** FlipKey is a vacation rental platform owned by TripAdvisor that focuses exclusively on vacation rentals and provides hosts with tools to list and manage their properties. FlipKey benefits from TripAdvisor's large user base and offers features such as guest reviews and communication tools.

- **Rentalo:** Rentalo, a platform specifically designed for vacation rentals, allows hosts to list their properties and connect with travelers seeking accommodations. It offers various features, including a booking management system and lead generation tools.

When choosing online sites to list your vacation home, consider the platform's user base, reach, features, and fees. It may be beneficial to list your property on multiple platforms to maximize exposure and increase the chances of attracting guests. Additionally, consider regional or local vacation rental platforms that may cater to specific markets or niches.

ONLINE MARKETING TECHNIQUES

The first step in marketing your rental on these platforms is creating a compelling listing with high-quality photos. In addition to your listing, most platforms allow you to build a host profile, which is an opportunity to build trust with potential guests. Highlight your commitment to providing a great guest experience and respond promptly and professionally to any guest reviews or comments.

Price competitively, but don't undersell your property. Research other rentals in your area to get an idea of the going rate, and consider employing dynamic pricing, adjusting your rates based on demand, season, and local events.

Remember to keep your calendar up to date. An accurate calendar not only helps prevent double bookings but also helps your property appear in the right searches. If guests see that your property is consistently unavailable or booked, they might pass it by.

It's also a good idea to diversify the platforms you list on to increase your exposure. Each platform has its own user base and unique features, so listing on multiple sites can help you reach a wider audience.

Keep in mind that each platform also has its own rules and fee structures, so make sure you understand these before you list your property.

Online platforms and listing sites can be powerful tools for marketing your short-term vacation rental, but success requires a well-crafted listing, high-quality photos, competitive pricing, and good host practices.

PROPERTY PHOTOS THAT SELL

High-quality images can capture the attention of potential guests browsing through countless listings and can significantly influence their decision to book. The goal is not only to accurately represent your property but also to create an emotional connection that entices viewers to imagine themselves in the space.

Take some time to go to one of the online listing sites and look at the photography used by the different owners. You will see a glaring difference between the exceptionally good photos and the very average photos. Now take a guess on who is booking more nights!

To start, consider hiring a professional real estate photographer. They have the experience and equipment necessary to capture the property in its best light, literally and figuratively. And they understand the importance of staging, angles, and lighting, which can dramatically affect the quality of the final image.

If your budget doesn't allow for a professional photographer, invest in a decent camera and learn some basic photography techniques. However, spending some money now for professional photos will provide you with significantly more rentals, which means more revenue.

Before shooting, prepare your home thoroughly. Clean and declutter each room, removing personal items and anything that could be a distraction in the photos. Stage each space with the guest experience in mind. This might include setting the dining table, fluffing up cushions on the couch, or turning on the fireplace. Remember, you're not just selling a space; you're selling an experience.

Lighting is paramount when it comes to photography. Natural light is typically the most flattering, so aim to take your photos during the day, ideally during the 'golden hours' just after sunrise or before sunset when the light is soft and warm. Make sure all lights are on and blinds or curtains are open to let in as much light as possible. Avoid using flash as it can create harsh shadows and make the space look less welcoming.

Take multiple photos from different angles of each room, as well as the exterior of the property and any outdoor spaces. Don't forget to include photos of unique features or amenities. Your photos should tell a story and give potential guests a virtual tour of the space.

Once the photos are taken, some post-processing might be necessary to adjust lighting, contrast, and color balance. There are numerous software options available for this, many of which are quite user-friendly. Remember, the goal is to enhance the images, not to misrepresent the property.

Lastly, make sure your photos are optimized for the online platforms you're using. Each platform has its own guidelines for image size and format, so ensure your photos meet these to avoid them being cropped or distorted.

VIRTUAL TOURS

In addition to offering professional photos, you can also create a virtual tour for your vacation home. Creating a virtual tour is an excellent marketing strategy that can significantly increase the appeal of your property. A virtual tour provides potential guests with an immersive, 360-degree view of your property, giving them a better sense of the layout, space, and atmosphere than traditional photos can. This allows them to visualize themselves in the space, increasing their confidence in their booking decision.

To begin creating a virtual tour, you'll need a 360-degree camera or a smartphone equipped with a 360-degree photo app. With a range of prices and features, you can easily find one that fits your budget and has the resolution and quality to create clear, detailed images. Or, when searching for your photographer, find one who offers both still image and virtual tour services. Utilizing professional photographers gets the best results and is absolutely worth the money.

Once you've captured all your images, you'll need to stitch them together to create a 360-degree view. Some cameras come with their own software to do this, but if yours doesn't, you can use third-party software. This can be a complex process, so you might consider hiring a professional if it's beyond your technical abilities.

Most major vacation rental platforms support virtual tours. If your platform doesn't, you can host the tour on a separate site and link to it from your listing, just make sure to highlight the virtual tour in your property description to draw potential guests' attention to it.

With a virtual tour, you're providing an interactive, realistic view of your property that can help set you apart from other listings, impress potential guests, and ultimately lead to more bookings.

CREATING A COMPELLING LISTING

A great listing not only accurately presents your rental, but also creates an inviting picture of what a stay at your property would be like, enticing potential guests to book.

Begin with a strong, descriptive title that immediately captures the attention of potential guests. The title should give a clear sense of what your property offers, whether it's the location ("Sunny Beachfront Bungalow"), unique features ("Rustic Cabin with Private Hot Tub"), or the ambiance ("Cozy Mountain Retreat").

The description should paint a picture of your property and its surroundings, capturing the imagination of potential guests. Highlight unique selling points, the layout and decor of the property, and key features and amenities. Describe the atmosphere and character of the property and the experience it offers. However, be sure to keep the information accurate and avoid exaggeration. Misrepresenting your property could lead to dissatisfied guests and negative reviews.

Don't forget to detail all the amenities your property offers. This includes practical items like Wi-Fi, washer and dryer, air conditioning, as well as luxury touches like a hot tub, pool, or high-end kitchen appliances. If you offer additional services such as complimentary Netflix or a stocked pantry, mention these, too.

Also, provide a detailed and accurate description of the location and the neighborhood. Mention proximity to popular attractions, restaurants, shopping, and public transportation. If your property offers stunning views, is in a quiet locale, or is a stone's throw away from a buzzing nightlife, be sure to mention it. Access is critical to vacation home users, so give them good details on getting to the places they want to go.

Include clear and detailed information about practical aspects such as check-in and check-out times, your cancellation policy, and any house rules. This helps guests know what to expect and may reduce the number of questions you have to answer.

A compelling listing requires a balance of appealing and accurate descriptions, high-quality photos, and excellent customer service. With these in place, your vacation home will be well on its way to becoming a popular choice for vacationers.

PERFECT PRICING STRATEGIES

Utilizing perfect pricing strategies and optimizing rental rates will have an impact on your marketability and ability to be competitive when booking your vacation home. The right pricing strategy not only ensures profitability but also enhances the competitiveness of your property in the market.

Optimizing rental rates for your vacation property is crucial for maximizing revenue and occupancy. Here are some pricing strategies to consider.

Market Research

Conduct thorough market research to understand pricing trends, demand patterns, and competitor rates in your vacation rental's location. Analyze similar properties in the area and consider factors such as property type, size, amenities, location, and guest reviews when comparing prices.

Seasonal Pricing

Adjust your rental rates based on seasonal demand. Set higher rates during peak seasons or holidays when demand is higher. During off-peak seasons, consider offering discounted rates or promotions to attract more bookings. Be mindful of local events, festivals, or other factors that may influence demand.

Dynamic Pricing

Dynamic pricing strategies adjust rates in response to changing demand, supply, or market conditions. Consider using automated pricing tools or software that can analyze data in real-time and optimize rates based on factors such as occupancy, booking trends, and market demand.

Length of Stay Discounts

Encourage longer bookings by offering discounts or incentives for extended stays. Set tiered pricing structures where guests receive a reduced nightly rate for booking a certain number of nights. This can attract guests seeking longer vacations or those who prefer the convenience of a single booking.

Understanding your property's position in the market is crucial. One of the first places to start is by researching similar properties in your area, looking at their prices, occupancy rates, amenities, and guest reviews. This will give you an idea of the price range for properties like yours. Keep in mind that prices can vary greatly based on factors such as location, property size, and amenities.

A dynamic pricing strategy can be beneficial, allowing you to adjust prices based on demand. During peak seasons or popular events, you can raise prices, whereas during off-peak times, lowering prices can help maintain occupancy rates. Remember, it's often better to rent your property at a lower rate than to have it sitting vacant.

Aim to strike a balance between maximizing your revenue and maintaining competitive rates. Overpricing can lead to low occupancy, while underpricing could mean leaving money on the table. Regularly reviewing and adjusting your pricing strategy can help maintain this balance.

Consider the psychological impact of pricing. Pricing your property at $99 instead of $100, for instance, can make it appear more affordable. Additionally, offering discounts for longer stays can attract guests looking for extended vacations and reduce turnover costs.

Investing in a revenue management tool can also be beneficial. These tools use data to predict market demand and suggest optimal pricing, taking into account factors such as seasonality, local events, and market trends.

There are also several services available that offer dynamic pricing strategies tailored to short-term vacation rentals, like Beyond Pricing, PriceLabs, and Wheelhouse. These services use sophisticated algorithms to analyze market data and trends in real time, considering factors such as seasonality, local events, weekdays, weekends, and even the changing booking patterns caused by variables like weather conditions or a global pandemic. They automatically adjust your rental rates accordingly, aiming to maximize your revenue and occupancy.

It's important to note, however, that while these tools provide valuable insights and automation, they are not a substitute for understanding your unique property and market. It's crucial to review the suggested prices and make manual adjustments when necessary. These tools usually charge a percentage of the booking revenue or a fixed monthly fee, so you'll need to factor this into your budgeting.

It is also important to be transparent about your prices and fees. Hidden costs can lead to negative reviews and damage your reputation. Ensure that cleaning fees, service fees, and any other costs are clearly outlined in your listing.

The right pricing strategy is a delicate balance of various factors. It requires continuous research, adjustment, and a deep understanding of your market. However, when done correctly, it can significantly enhance the profitability and success of your short-term vacation home rental.

BUILDING A WEBSITE THAT CONVERTS

In the age of digital marketing, having a well-crafted, attractive website for your short-term vacation rental is not a luxury, but a necessity. An effective website not only enhances your property's online presence but also serves as a powerful marketing tool that can increase bookings and drive business growth.

The first major benefit of having a dedicated website is credibility. A well-designed, professional-looking website can instill confidence in potential renters and convey the seriousness and legitimacy of your vacation rental business. It acts as the digital storefront for your property, providing visitors with their first impression of what to expect.

A website also provides a centralized platform for showcasing your property. Here you can display high-resolution photos, virtual tours, detailed descriptions of the property and its amenities, guest reviews, and any other information you deem necessary. Unlike listing platforms where you are restricted to their format and rules, on your website, you have complete control over content and presentation.

Another significant benefit is direct bookings. While listing sites are useful, they often charge fees for bookings made through their platform. By offering the possibility to book directly through your website, you can avoid these fees and increase your revenue. A simple, user-friendly booking and payment system is crucial for this.

Additionally, having a website improves your visibility on search engines. With the right search engine optimization (SEO) strategies, such as using relevant keywords and regularly updating your site with fresh content, your website can rank higher in search results, making it easier for potential guests to find your property.

A website also enables you to engage more effectively with your guests. You can add a blog to share updates, local travel tips, or news about your property. Integrating social media can also help create a community around your property, boosting customer engagement and retention.

You can even use your website to collect visitor emails for your marketing efforts. By offering website visitors something of value, like a travel guide to your location in exchange for their email address, you can build an email list for sending promotional offers, updates, and newsletters.

A well-designed and effectively managed website is a powerful tool that can significantly enhance your short-term vacation rental marketing strategy. Not only does it offer a platform for showcasing your property in the best possible light, but it also provides opportunities for direct bookings, improved search engine visibility, greater customer engagement, and valuable data collection.

SEO OPTIMIZATION

Having a well-optimized website is crucial to making your short-term vacation rental property more visible to potential guests. Search engine optimization (SEO) is the process of improving a website's visibility for relevant searches, and it is an essential component of any successful digital marketing strategy.

Firstly, keyword research is vital. Identify the keywords potential guests might use when searching for a vacation rental like yours; they could be related to the location, the type of property, the amenities you offer, or other unique selling points. Once you've identified these keywords, incorporate them naturally into your website content, including titles, descriptions, headers, and image alt tags.

Having a mobile-friendly website is also essential for SEO because more and more travelers are using their mobile devices to research and book accommodations. Google takes mobile responsiveness into account when ranking websites, so ensure that your site is easily navigable and looks good on all device types and screen sizes.

Website speed is another critical factor. Users and search engines favor sites that load quickly. You can improve your site speed by optimizing your images, using a reliable web host, and minimizing the use of heavy scripts and unnecessary plugins.

Additionally, having fresh, unique, and valuable content on your website can significantly improve your SEO. Regularly update your website with blog posts about local attractions, tips for travelers, or other relevant topics that your potential guests might find interesting. This can not only improve your rankings, but also position you as an expert, thereby instilling more trust in your potential guests.

Backlinks, or links from other websites to yours, can also help improve your SEO. They serve as a vote of confidence in your website from other webmasters. Reach out to local businesses, tourism boards, or bloggers and see if they'd be willing to link to your site. Additionally, you can list your property on relevant directories or local listings.

By implementing these strategies, you can improve your website's SEO, making it easier for potential guests to discover your short-term vacation home rental. It's a long-term process that requires regular tweaking and refinement, but the rewards in increased visibility and bookings are well worth the effort.

CREATING A GUEST EXPERIENCE

Creating an unforgettable guest experience for a short-term vacation home rental is about more than just providing a place to sleep. It is about creating an experience that is comfortable, unique, and leaves your guests eager to return or recommend your property to others.

The process begins from the moment a guest discovers your property. By making the booking process simple and convenient and communicating promptly and professionally with the guests to answer their queries, you create a great first impression.

The guest experience also includes the check-in process. Some hosts choose to meet their guests personally, offering a warm welcome and introducing them to the property. Others prefer a self check-in method, providing clear instructions on how to access the property. Regardless of the method you choose, ensure that the process is smooth and hassle-free.

The property itself plays a significant role in the guest experience. It should be clean, well-maintained, and stocked with all the essential amenities. Little touches like a well-equipped kitchen or a welcome basket with local treats can make a big difference.

And I cannot even begin to tell you how important the bed and bedding are. There is nothing worse than showing up to relax and rejuvenate on your vacation, only to receive poor sleep due to the poor sleeping amenities. This is an area where we will always spend additional money.

The property should also reflect the unique selling points you highlighted in your listing, whether it's a stunning view, local artwork, or a hot tub.

Information about the local area can also enhance the guest experience. Provide a guidebook or a list of recommendations for local attractions, restaurants, and events. This not only saves your guests time researching but also helps them feel like locals during their stay.

Communication is key throughout the guest's stay. Make sure your guests know how to reach you if they have any issues or questions. Respond promptly to any communication and be proactive in solving any problems that arise.

The check-out process should be as smooth as the check-in. Provide clear instructions on what the guests need to do before leaving and thank them for choosing your property. After they've left, reach out with a thank-you note and invite them to review their stay.

Remember, creating a memorable guest experience is an ongoing process. Continually seek feedback from your guests and use it to improve your service. The more effort you put into making your guests' stay enjoyable, the more likely they are to return and recommend your vacation rental to others.

OFFERING A GUIDEBOOK

Offering a guidebook for your short-term vacation home rental can greatly enhance the guest experience. It can serve as a valuable resource for guests, providing them with useful information and tips about your rental property and its surroundings.

A comprehensive guidebook should start with a warm welcome message and introduction. Then, it should thoroughly explain the important details of your property, including how to operate the appliances, the Wi-Fi password, how to adjust the thermostat, and any house rules that the guests should be aware of. It is also a good idea to include emergency contact information, such as your number and the local police, fire department, and hospital details.

However, a guidebook is not just about the property. It should also include a wealth of information about the local area as well. This could consist of recommendations for restaurants and cafes, nearby attractions, local parks, and outdoor activities. Providing guests with your personal suggestions can give them a local's perspective and help them make the most out of their stay.

It is a good practice to include practical information such as the locations of the nearest supermarket, pharmacy, and gas station, as well as public transportation information, if applicable. This information can be particularly helpful for guests who are not familiar with the area or are visiting from abroad.

If there are unique or lesser-known attractions in your area, be sure to highlight these in your guidebook. This could include everything from hidden hiking trails to local artisan markets, lesser-known museums, or the best spots to watch the sunset. Highlighting these unique features can help set your property apart from others.

Consider also including a section about local events and festivals. If there are events happening in your area during your guests' stay, they'll appreciate being in the know.

Always present your guidebook in an appealing, easy-to-read format. Include photos where possible and organize the information logically. You can choose to provide a physical copy at your property or a digital version that guests can access on their devices, or both.

A well-crafted guidebook is more than just a handy tool for guests— it's an opportunity to elevate their experience, make them feel cared for, and introduce them to the best your local area has to offer. By investing time and thought into creating a thorough and personalized guidebook, you'll be providing a valuable service that can help set your vacation rental apart.

COLLABORATING WITH LOCAL BUSINESSES

Collaborating with local businesses can be an effective way to enhance the value proposition of your short-term vacation rental, while also fostering a sense of community and supporting the local economy. There are several ways to approach this kind of partnership, each with its own potential benefits.

One common strategy is to arrange for discounts or special deals for your guests at local businesses. For example, you might reach out to a popular restaurant, a spa, or a tour operator and ask if they would be willing to offer a small discount to guests who mention that they're staying at your property. In this win-win situation, your guests get a special deal which makes their stay more enjoyable, and the business gets additional customers.

You could also consider creating bundled experiences or packages. These might involve collaborating with a local tour operator to offer guided tours of the area, or with a local chef to offer private cooking classes.

For example, having a local massage therapist or chef that can come directly to the home and provide their services is both convenient and also adds to the overall vacation experience. This not only gives your guests unique experiences they wouldn't get elsewhere but also helps them see the value in booking your property over another.

Another strategy could involve featuring local products in your rental. This might involve sourcing locally made soaps for the bathroom, providing local coffee or tea in the kitchen, or featuring local artwork throughout the property. Not only does this give your guests a more authentic experience, but it can also help support local artisans and small businesses.

Collaboration can extend to marketing efforts as well. Partner with local businesses to co-promote each other's offerings. They can mention your vacation rental to their customers, and you can return the favor by highlighting their business on your website or in your rental.

By collaborating with local businesses, you can enhance the guest experience, support the local economy, and contribute to your property's distinctiveness. Plus, it can be a powerful marketing tool, as it shows that your property is connected and engaged with the local community.

CUSTOMER FEEDBACK

Customer feedback from guests can provide invaluable insights into the guest experience and help you make informed decisions about potential improvements, leading to higher customer satisfaction and repeat business.

The first key step in using customer feedback effectively is creating a system that encourages guests to provide their thoughts and comments. This can be accomplished by sending a follow-up email after their stay, asking them to review their experience. You could also leave a guest book at the property, which not only invites feedback but also allows guests to share their experiences with future visitors.

Once you receive feedback, it is crucial to review it carefully. Look for common trends or recurring issues that multiple guests mention. Perhaps several guests have noted that the kitchen could be better stocked, or the Wi-Fi signal is weak in certain areas of the home. These recurring themes can highlight areas for improvement that you might not have noticed.

Also, pay attention to the positive feedback. Positive comments can highlight what you're doing right and what guests appreciate the most about your vacation rental. For example, if guests frequently praise the comfortable beds, the stunning view, or the convenient location, you can emphasize these aspects in your marketing materials to attract future guests.

Responding to feedback is equally important. Whether a review is positive or negative, take the time to reply in a thoughtful and professional manner. Thank guests for their positive reviews and show appreciation for their comments. Make sure they know their opinion matters and their feedback is appreciated.

For any negative feedback, address the concerns raised, apologize if necessary, and assure the guest that you'll look into the matter. This shows prospective guests that you take their feedback seriously and are committed to providing a great experience.

Lastly, it's important to implement changes based on the feedback received. If guests have highlighted issues that can be fixed, make it a priority to address these problems. Then, let your guests know that their feedback has led to tangible improvements. This not only improves your property but also builds trust with your guests, as it shows that you value their input.

By encouraging feedback, reviewing it carefully, responding appropriately, and making improvements based on the input received, you can continually enhance your property and the guest experience.

SUPERHOST STATUS

Achieving Superhost status for your short-term vacation home rental can significantly enhance your rental property's visibility and reputation. Superhost is a program run by Airbnb, one of the leading online marketplaces for lodging and tourism experiences. The Superhost status is awarded to hosts who consistently deliver excellent service and receive high ratings from their guests.

Airbnb assesses potential Superhosts quarterly, evaluating the following criteria: hosts must have hosted at least ten stays in the past year or, if they offer long-term stays, have completed three stays that total at least 100 nights; they must have a 90% response rate or higher for all messages; they must have a cancellation rate of 1% or less, barring extenuating circumstances; and they must have received a five-star review for at least 80% of the stays.

Achieving Superhost status offers several advantages. Your listing will have a Superhost badge, which can make your property stand out to prospective guests and indicate that you offer excellent service. According to Airbnb, Superhosts tend to earn more than other hosts, as the Superhost badge can attract more guests and allow hosts to charge a premium for their proven service.

Superhosts also receive enhanced visibility in search results and priority customer support from Airbnb. In addition, they get exclusive rewards, such as travel credits and discounts as a thank-you for their commitment to providing exceptional hospitality.

Maintaining Superhost status requires consistent effort as you'll need to continue meeting Airbnb's performance standards each time they assess eligibility. However, the benefits it brings make it a worthwhile goal for any host.

Achieving and maintaining Superhost status can significantly enhance the success of your short-term vacation home rental. It not only bolsters your reputation and visibility but can also lead to increased income and other exclusive benefits. Ultimately, the key to achieving Superhost status lies in consistently providing excellent service to your guests.

GETTING THE FIVE-STAR REVIEW

In the world of short-term vacation home rentals, a steady flow of five-star reviews can significantly boost your property's visibility, increase its appeal to potential guests, and consequently raise your earnings. Garnering top reviews isn't about luck, but rather the result of thoughtful management and a customer-centered approach.

Set clear expectations for your guests from the outset. Your listing should be accurate and honest, detailing not only the features and amenities of your property but also any potential drawbacks. Guests appreciate knowing exactly what they are booking, and there's nothing more damaging to your rating than disappointed guests who feel they were misled.

Next, focus on cleanliness. A sparkling, clean property is one of the first things guests will notice upon arrival, and it significantly influences their overall impression of your rental. Consider hiring professional cleaning services to ensure the highest level of cleanliness.

Providing excellent communication is also key. From the moment guests book your property, keep the lines of communication open. Respond promptly to inquiries and provide all necessary information for their stay. Make check-in and check-out processes seamless, and be available to handle any issues that might arise during their stay.

Another significant role in the overall guest experience is amenities. Invest in quality furnishings and ensure that your rental is well-stocked with essentials such as towels, toiletries, cooking equipment, and a reliable internet connection. Extra touches, like a coffee maker with pods, a bottle of wine, or a list of local recommendations, can make guests feel valued and well-cared for.

Fast, reliable Wi-Fi is also essential in today's connected world. Many guests rely on internet access for entertainment, keeping in touch with family, or even working remotely. If your Wi-Fi is poor or unreliable, it could significantly impact your reviews.

Lastly, ask for reviews. While many guests will leave a review voluntarily, others may forget or not realize how vital their feedback is. After their stay, send a friendly message thanking them for choosing your rental and asking them to leave a review if they enjoyed their stay.

By setting clear expectations, maintaining high standards of cleanliness, providing excellent communication and amenities, ensuring reliable Wi-Fi, and politely asking for reviews, you can boost your chances of receiving consistent five-star reviews for your short-term vacation home rental.

LAST-MINUTE BOOKINGS

The ability to provide last-minute bookings for a short-term vacation home rental can open up an entirely new customer base and increase your overall revenue. It can attract impulsive vacationers, business travelers with sudden trips, or people facing unexpected circumstances that require immediate accommodations.

However, providing last-minute bookings requires careful planning and exceptional efficiency. The key to managing last-minute bookings successfully is ensuring that your property is always ready to receive guests. This means maintaining high standards of cleanliness and comfort at all times, as you may not have a large window between bookings for thorough cleaning and restocking of essentials. Hiring a reliable cleaning service that offers on-demand cleaning could be invaluable.

When offering last-minute bookings, it is critical that you streamline your check-in process as much as possible. Automated check-in systems like smart locks or lockboxes can allow guests to check in immediately, which is often a crucial factor for last-minute bookings. Provide clear and concise instructions to your guests for a smooth self-check-in experience.

From a marketing perspective, make it clear in your property listing that you accept last-minute bookings. You could offer discounted rates for last-minute bookings, as they may otherwise stay vacant. However, make sure to balance this strategy with your financial objectives, as too heavy discounts can impact your profitability.

You should also build an email list of people who are looking to know when you have a last-minute discounted opportunity available. There are people who like to do last-minute travel and are always looking for a good discount!

Having a robust property management system is also crucial. It should be capable of instantly updating your property's availability across all platforms whenever a booking is made. This way, you can avoid the risk of double bookings and ensure that your calendar is always up-to-date enabling guests to make last-minute bookings confidently.

Even with last-minute bookings, guest communication remains essential. Ensure that you are easily reachable and can respond to inquiries promptly. Communicate all necessary information regarding their stay as soon as the booking is made. The ability to provide swift and effective customer service can greatly improve your guests' overall experience, leading to positive reviews and possibly repeat bookings.

While offering last-minute bookings can require more administrative work and quick turnarounds, it can also lead to increased revenue and occupancy rates. By optimizing your operations and maintaining strong guest communication, you can successfully cater to last-minute bookings in your short-term vacation home rental.

SOCIAL MEDIA MARKETING

Social media has become an integral part of many people's daily lives and a powerful marketing tool for businesses, including short-term vacation home rentals. It provides a platform where you can connect with your audience, increase your rental's visibility, share updates, and promote your property.

The first step in social media marketing is to determine which platforms your target audience uses most. Platforms like Facebook and Instagram are often popular choices due to their large user bases and visual focus, which is perfect for showcasing your property. However, depending on your target demographic, platforms such as Pinterest, LinkedIn, or Twitter may also be relevant.

After choosing your platforms, you need to create engaging content. High-quality photos are a must in the vacation rental business. Show off your property's best features, the beautiful views, unique amenities, or any recent upgrades or renovations. Videos are also highly engaging and could include a walkthrough of the property, a highlight reel of local attractions, or testimonials from happy guests.

In addition to property-related content, consider sharing posts that provide value to your audience and align with their interests, such as local travel tips, event announcements, or recommendations for local restaurants or attractions. This helps to position you not just as a rental property, but as a knowledgeable local guide.

Encourage engagement on your posts by asking questions, running contests, or requesting that your followers share their favorite memories from their stay at your property. The more your audience interacts with your posts, the greater the reach of your content.

Remember to respond promptly to comments or messages on your social platforms. This not only helps to build relationships with potential guests but also shows that you're attentive and responsive, which can boost your reputation.

You can also consider paid advertising options such as Facebook or Instagram ads. These can be targeted based on a variety of factors, including location, interests, age, and more, allowing you to reach potential guests who are most likely to be interested in your rental.

Finally, make sure that you are tracking your social media efforts. Most platforms offer analytics that can help you understand which posts are performing well and why. Use this information to refine your social media strategy, focus on the content that resonates most with your audience, and ultimately drive more bookings for your vacation home rental.

When used effectively, social media can be a powerful marketing tool for your short-term vacation home rental, helping you to increase visibility, engage with potential guests, and drive more bookings.

KPIS AND ANALYTICS

All good businesses do an excellent job of monitoring and analyzing the performance of their marketing efforts. They also have a good understanding of the key performance indicators (KPIs) and analytics that determine the success and impact the profitability and revenue streams for their short-term vacation home rental so they know what's working and what's not. This allows them to make informed decisions and refine their strategies to increase bookings and maximize profits.

Start by defining your KPIs . These could be the number of bookings, revenue, average occupancy rate, average daily rate, or guest satisfaction ratings. Having clear KPIs will give you a way to measure the success of your marketing efforts objectively.

Next, make use of analytics tools available to you. Many online platforms, like Google Analytics, Airbnb, VRBO, and social media sites, provide detailed analytics that can help you understand how your property is performing. For instance, you can track website traffic, booking sources, demographic information about your guests, and the performance of your social media posts.

Pay particular attention to the conversion rate, which is the percentage of people who book your property after visiting your website or viewing your listing on a rental platform. A low conversion rate could indicate problems with your listing or pricing.

Also, monitor the performance of any paid advertising campaigns you're running, whether they're on social media, search engines, or rental platforms. Track the return on investment (ROI) for each campaign to see if they're worth the cost.

It is also extremely important to pay attention to the feedback and reviews from your guests. While these aren't quantitative metrics, they can provide valuable insights into what guests love about your property and areas where you can improve. Negative reviews, while not pleasant, can be particularly informative as they highlight areas that need attention.

Also, don't forget to benchmark your performance against similar properties in your area. This can help you identify where you're outperforming your competition and where you might need to step up your game.

Remember, the goal of monitoring and analyzing your marketing performance isn't just to collect data. It's to gain insights that you can use to improve your marketing efforts, enhance the guest experience, and ultimately increase your profits. This is a continuous process that should be an integral part of your overall business strategy.

Marketing your short-term vacation home rental is an essential aspect of your investment plan. With an effective marketing strategy, your vacation home rental can stand out in a competitive market and continue to deliver profitable returns.

CHAPTER 11

MANAGING YOUR VACATION HOME

The way you manage your vacation home will often come down to personal preference and the time you have available to effectively handle the responsibilities required to successfully manage your investment.

Some property owners enjoy the hands-on aspect of managing their property and have specific expectations regarding the quality of service and the maintenance they prefer to handle themselves. Others prefer to outsource these tasks so they can focus on other things.

Deciding how to manage your vacation home isn't a one-time decision. You can try different approaches to see what works best for you and your property. Ultimately, the goal should be to provide a great experience for your guests while making the process manageable for you.

When deciding how to manage your vacation home, there are several key factors that you should take into consideration.

Time Commitment

Managing a vacation property can be time-consuming, particularly if it is a short-term rental. Tasks include marketing, handling reservations and payments, managing housekeeping and maintenance, addressing guest inquiries and complaints, and dealing with emergencies. You'll need to consider whether you have the time and availability to handle these tasks effectively or if you need outside help.

Proximity to Property

If you live far from your vacation property, managing it personally can be challenging. In such cases, hiring a property management company or a local caretaker can be a more practical solution.

Knowledge and Experience

Managing a vacation rental requires knowledge of the local real estate market, an understanding of relevant laws and regulations, experience with marketing and customer service, and familiarity with property maintenance and repairs. If you lack expertise in these areas, you may benefit from professional help.

Financial Considerations

Hiring a property management company will cost money, typically a percentage of the rental income. You'll need to weigh this cost against the potential benefits in terms of time saved, increased occupancy rates, and higher guest satisfaction.

Legal and Regulatory Considerations

Depending on the location of your property, there may be specific rules and regulations related to vacation rentals. These can include licensing requirements, tax implications, and regulations on short-term rentals, and each of these factors can impact management decisions.

Technology Comfort Level

Many aspects of vacation rental management, such as booking systems, customer communication, and payment processing, are now handled online. If you're comfortable using this technology, self-management might be more feasible.

Setting Up a Property Management System

Setting up a management system for a vacation property involves several steps to ensure efficient operations and a smooth guest experience. Here's a general guide on how to set up a property management system:

Determine your goals and objectives for the vacation property, then clarify whether you plan to manage the property yourself or hire a property management company. Identify your target market, desired rental rates, occupancy goals, and any specific services or amenities you want to offer.

Next, select a property management software that suits your needs. Look for features such as reservation management, calendar synchronization, guest communication tools, financial tracking, and reporting capabilities. Popular property management software options include platforms like Airbnb, HomeAway, VRBO, or dedicated vacation rental software like Guesty, Lodgify, or Kigo.

PROPERTY MANAGEMENT OPTIONS

Your choice of management depends on your preferences, availability, expertise, and desired level of involvement. Some common management options for vacation rental investments include

Self-Management

Self-managing your short-term vacation rental investment can be rewarding but also demanding. This approach allows you to retain control over every aspect of the rental process, potentially maximizing your returns by avoiding management fees. However, it also requires a considerable commitment of time, energy, and resources.

One of the main advantages of self-management is the level of control it provides. As the owner and manager, you decide on the rental rates, marketing strategies, guest selection, and housekeeping standards. You'll also have direct communication with your guests, enabling you to provide personalized service and manage their expectations which can lead to better reviews and increased repeat bookings.

On the financial side, self-management allows you to avoid paying property management fees, which can often range from 10%—30% of the rental income. This means that all rental income, after expenses, goes directly to you. However, you will need to consider the time and costs involved in advertising, maintenance, repairs, customer service, and compliance with local regulations.

A major consideration in self-management is your proximity to the rental property. If you live nearby, you can respond quickly to any issues that arise, such as maintenance emergencies or guest concerns. If you live far away, however, these tasks become much more challenging.

Technology can greatly assist in self-management. Various property management software and online platforms can automate booking, payment processing, and guest communication which can save you time and make the management process more efficient.

Despite these advantages, self-management also comes with challenges. It requires a broad range of skills, from customer service and marketing to maintenance and accounting. There's also a significant time commitment involved, especially if your property has high turnover.

With its financial advantages and full control over the rental process, self-managing a short-term vacation rental can be a good option if you have the time, skills, and inclination to take on the various tasks involved. However, it's also a significant commitment and requires a readiness to handle any issues that may arise, so you need to make sure you evaluate all aspects.

Hybrid or Co-Host Management

A hybrid or co-host management model offers a middle ground for owners of short-term vacation rentals. In this approach, the property owner and a co-host share the responsibilities of managing the property, but the specific duties each party takes on can vary greatly depending on the agreement.

Co-hosting can be an excellent option if you need help managing your property but don't want to relinquish full control to a property management company. With a co-host, you can share the workload while maintaining a degree of personal involvement in managing your property. This could be especially helpful if you live far away from your rental property or if you simply don't have the time to manage all aspects of it.

In a typical co-hosting arrangement, you might handle certain tasks such as setting rental rates, marketing the property, and communicating with guests before their stay. Your co-host, who is often a local person or company, might manage on-the-ground tasks such as key exchange, housekeeping, maintenance issues, and responding to guests' needs during their stay.

One of the key benefits of a hybrid or co-host management model is that it can be customized to your needs and preferences. You can choose to take on the tasks you enjoy or are good at, and delegate the rest to your co-host.

However, there are some factors to consider. Firstly, good communication between you and your co-host is crucial to ensure a seamless experience for your guests. Secondly, while a co-host will typically charge less than a full-service property management company, there will still be a cost involved, which needs to be factored into your budget.

Overall, a hybrid or co-host management model offers a flexible solution that can be tailored to the unique needs and circumstances of each property owner. It can be an effective way to lighten the load of managing a short-term vacation rental, while still allowing you to maintain a level of control and involvement.

Professional Property Management

Professional property management is a popular option for owners who prefer a hands-off approach or lack the time, expertise, or proximity to effectively manage their property. Hiring a professional property management company can alleviate the burden of day-to-day tasks and provide numerous benefits.

One of the main advantages of professional property management is expertise. Property management companies have experience and knowledge of the local rental market. They understand pricing trends, can advise on optimizing rental rates, and have insights into effective marketing strategies to attract guests. Their expertise can help maximize your rental income and occupancy rates.

Property management companies also handle the operational aspects of renting out your property. They take care of listing creation and distribution across various platforms, responding to guest inquiries, managing reservations, and handling the check-in and check-out process. They can also coordinate cleaning and maintenance services, ensuring your property is in top condition for each guest's arrival.

Another significant benefit is their ability to provide round-the-clock guest support. Property management companies have dedicated customer service teams available 24/7 to address guest inquiries, handle emergencies, and resolve any issues that may arise during a guest's stay. This level of support can enhance the guest experience, leading to positive reviews and repeat bookings.

Professional property managers also have systems in place for financial management. They can handle rental payments, collect security deposits, and provide detailed financial reports, making it easier for you to track income and expenses. This level of transparency can be invaluable for your financial records and tax purposes.

The fees typically range from 10% to 30% of the rental income, depending on the services provided and the location of the property. It's important to carefully review the management agreement and understand the services included to ensure you're getting value for your money. While hiring a property management company incurs costs, it can be a worthwhile investment.

However, one of the disadvantages of a property management company is the control over the process that you relinquish. Nobody can possibly care about your property like you do. When you hire a property management company, you become one of many. There are very good management companies out there, but it is critical to find one that will give your property the attention that it deserves.

Professional property management can provide peace of mind and convenience for short-term vacation rental owners. The expertise, operational support, guest services, and financial management provided by property management companies can help optimize your rental property's performance and allow you to enjoy the benefits of passive income without the stress of day-to-day management.

Rental Agency

Working with a rental agency is another management option and involves partnering with a local agency that specializes in managing and marketing vacation rentals. This arrangement can offer several benefits for property owners.

Rental agencies have an extensive network and established marketing channels to promote your property. Their dedicated marketing team focuses on attracting guests, optimizing rental rates, and maximizing occupancy. With their expertise in targeted advertising and leveraging online platforms, they can significantly increase your property's visibility and reach.

Additionally, rental agencies often have professional photography and copywriting services at their disposal. They can create compelling listings with high-quality photos and engaging descriptions that highlight your property's unique features and attract potential guests.

When it comes to guest management, rental agencies handle the entire rental process, including guest inquiries, reservations, and check-in/check-out procedures. They have systems in place to ensure smooth communication with guests and can handle any issues or concerns that arise during their stay. This level of professionalism can lead to positive guest experiences and help generate positive reviews for your property.

One significant advantage of rental agencies is their local presence and knowledge. They are familiar with the area, including popular attractions, local events, and amenities, which enables them to provide guests with valuable information and recommendations. They can also stay updated on local regulations and compliance requirements, ensuring that your property operates within the legal framework.

While rental agencies charge a commission or management fee, usually a percentage of the rental income, this cost is offset by the time and effort saved in managing the property independently. The expertise and resources provided by rental agencies can potentially result in higher occupancy rates and increased rental income.

However, it's important to choose a reputable rental agency that aligns with your goals and expectations. Be sure to research and interview multiple agencies, inquire about their track record, ask for references, and review their management agreement thoroughly before making a decision.

Rental agency management offers convenience, expertise, and marketing power for owners of short-term vacation rental investments. By leveraging the agency's network, marketing expertise, and local knowledge, you can optimize the performance of your property, increase occupancy rates, and provide a high level of service to your guests.

When selecting a management option, consider factors such as your availability, desired level of control, expertise, local regulations, the rental market in your area, and the financial implications. It can be helpful to research and interview multiple management companies or co-hosts to find the option that aligns with your goals and provides the level of service you require.

HIRING A PROPERTY MANAGER

When hiring a property manager for your vacation home, it is essential to follow best practices to ensure you find a qualified and reliable professional.

One of the first things you need to do is determine your specific needs and expectations from the property manager. Identify the tasks and responsibilities you want them to handle, such as guest communication, marketing, maintenance coordination, and financial management.

When you have compiled a job description, ask for recommendations from trusted sources, such as fellow vacation rental owners, local real estate agents, or industry professionals. These referrals can help you identify property managers who have a proven track record and a positive reputation.

When interviewing candidates to assess their qualifications, experience, and compatibility with your needs, ask about their background in vacation property management, their understanding of local regulations, and their approach to guest satisfaction and property maintenance. Request and check references of previous clients or employers. And speak with property owners who have worked with the candidate to gain insights into their performance, reliability, and professionalism.

It is important to take into consideration the property manager's experience in managing vacation rentals, particularly in your specific location or a similar market. Look for knowledge of local market dynamics, pricing strategies, marketing techniques, and guest management skills.

A good candidate will have strong communication and exceptional customer service skills. Evaluate their ability to handle guest inquiries and concerns promptly and professionally, and consider their proficiency in handling conflicts or challenging situations that may arise with guests.

Your manager should also be very familiar with property management software, channel management tools, and online booking platforms. A tech-savvy property manager can effectively handle online reservations, calendar management, and guest communication.

A diligent property manager needs to be able to properly conduct property inspections to ensure the vacation home is well-maintained and complies with established standards, as well as identify any damages that the previous tenant may have done to the home. They should also be capable of identifying maintenance needs, coordinating repairs, and addressing any issues promptly.

Since financial management is important to the success of your investment, a property manager should have a solid understanding of all financial aspects related to vacation rental properties. Be certain to evaluate their proficiency in financial management, including handling rental income, expense tracking, and generating accurate financial reports.

And lastly, pay attention to your instincts and intuition during the hiring process. Choose a property manager you feel comfortable working with and trust to take care of your vacation home. Our instincts may not always be 100% accurate, but they prove to be spot on most of the time.

By following these best practices and thoroughly evaluating potential property managers, you increase the likelihood of finding a capable professional who can efficiently manage your vacation property and ensure a positive experience for guests.

OVERSEEING PROPERTY MANAGERS

Once you have your property manager in place, it is important that you implement effective management oversight for maintaining the quality and success of your vacation home rental. Here are some best practices for overseeing the management of your vacation home.

Regular Communication

Maintain regular communication with your property manager. Schedule check-in meetings or calls to discuss the property's performance, guest feedback, maintenance updates, and any other relevant matters. Promptly address any concerns or questions that arise.

Review Financial Reports

Regularly review financial reports provided by your property manager. These reports should include income statements, expense breakdowns, occupancy rates, and any other relevant financial information. Assess the financial performance of your vacation home to ensure it aligns with your goals.

Monitor Guest Feedback

Stay updated on guest feedback and reviews received through various platforms or guest surveys. Analyze the feedback to identify areas of improvement and address any recurring issues. Use this feedback to refine your property's offerings and enhance the guest experience.

Property Inspections

Conduct periodic property inspections to ensure it meets your standards and remains well-maintained. This can be done in person or through virtual inspections using photos or video calls. Evaluate the property's condition, cleanliness, and adherence to your established guidelines.

Marketing and Advertising

Stay involved in the marketing and advertising efforts for your vacation home. Review the property's online listings, photos, and descriptions to ensure they accurately represent your property and attract potential guests. Collaborate with your property manager on marketing strategies and promotions.

Stay Informed about Market Trends

Stay updated on market trends, industry developments, and changes in local regulations that may impact your vacation home. Be aware of any new competition or opportunities that can enhance your property's performance.

Maintenance and Repairs

Regularly communicate with your property manager about maintenance and repair needs. Ensure they are promptly addressing any issues that arise and maintaining a network of reliable service providers. Establish protocols for handling emergencies and ensure appropriate insurance coverage is in place.

Stay Compliant with Regulations

Stay informed about local regulations and ensure your vacation home remains compliant. Stay up to date on any changes in short-term rental regulations, taxation requirements, safety standards, and licensing obligations. Collaborate with your property manager to ensure compliance with all applicable laws.

Regular Performance Reviews

Conduct periodic performance reviews with your property manager. Evaluate their performance against agreed-upon objectives, key performance indicators, and guest feedback. Provide constructive feedback, discuss areas for improvement, and recognize their achievements.

Continuous Improvement

Encourage ongoing improvement and innovation in managing your vacation home. Foster a culture of learning and staying up-to-date on industry best practices. Encourage your property manager to suggest improvements, explore new technologies, or implement strategies that can enhance the property's performance.

Remember, effective oversight requires a balance between providing guidance and giving your property manager autonomy to carry out their responsibilities. Regular and open communication, monitoring key performance indicators, and fostering a collaborative relationship with your property manager are essential for successful vacation home management oversight.

OBJECTIVES FOR YOUR PROPERTY MANAGEMENT SYSTEMS

Setting up a property management system for a short-term vacation rental is crucial for several reasons.

First, it provides organization and efficiency in managing your property. A well-designed system streamlines processes such as reservations, bookings, guest communication, and maintenance, allowing you to save time and effort. It ensures that essential tasks are automated or easily managed, enabling you to focus on providing a great guest experience and growing your rental business.

A property management system also helps you maintain professionalism and consistency in managing your vacation rental. By implementing standardized processes and procedures, you can ensure that guests receive consistent information, have clear expectations, and experience a seamless booking and stay process. This professionalism helps build trust with guests, enhances your property's reputation, and encourages positive reviews and repeat bookings.

A property management system will also assist in enabling effective financial management by helping you track rental income, manage expenses, and generate financial reports for tax purposes. With built-in payment systems and automated reminders, you can ensure timely and secure transactions, reducing the risk of errors or disputes.

Property management systems will provide valuable data and insights to optimize your rental business. It allows you to track occupancy rates, monitor booking patterns, and analyze guest feedback and reviews. This data can help you make informed decisions about pricing, marketing strategies, and property improvements, ultimately maximizing your rental income and guest satisfaction.

And one of the most important factors is that setting up a property management system contributes to a better guest experience. It allows you to provide prompt and accurate responses to guest inquiries, deliver essential information about check-in procedures and property amenities, and address any issues or concerns in a timely manner. This level of responsiveness and professionalism enhances guest satisfaction, encourages positive reviews, and promotes guest loyalty.

By defining the key objectives as stated above, you create a framework for decision-making and help align your management system with your overall goals

RESEARCH AND SELECT A PROPERTY MANAGEMENT SYSTEM

Once you have assessed your objectives for your property management system, it's time to research and select the one that will ensure smooth operations and maximize the success of your rental business. Here are several steps to help you in the process.

- **Your Needs:** Begin by identifying your specific needs, and goals. Consider the size of your rental property portfolio, the number of properties you manage, your desired level of automation, and the specific features you require to help you narrow down the options and focus on systems that align with your unique requirements.

- **Market Research:** Research and compare different property management systems available in the market. Look for systems that specialize in short-term vacation rentals and have a track record of success. Consider factors such as the system's reputation, user reviews, client testimonials, and the number of properties currently using the platform.

- **Features and Functionality:** Create a list of features and functionalities that are essential for your property management needs. This may include online booking and reservation management, channel management to sync property listings across multiple platforms, automated guest communication, reporting and analytics, and integration with payment processing systems. Assess how well each system meets your requirements and whether they offer scalability to accommodate your future growth.

- **Ease of Use and User Interface:** User-friendliness and an intuitive interface are important considerations. A property management system that is easy to navigate and use will save you time and minimize the learning curve.

- **Customer Support and Training:** Look for companies that provide responsive customer service, training resources, and ongoing support to assist you with any technical issues or questions you may have. Good customer support is essential to ensure a smooth implementation and address any challenges that may arise.

- **Consider Integration and Compatibility:** If you already use other tools or software for your vacation rental business, consider the compatibility and integration options with the property management system. Check if it can integrate with your existing systems such as channel managers, online booking platforms, accounting software, or dynamic pricing tools; integration capabilities can streamline your workflow and enhance efficiency.

- **Cost and Pricing Structure:** Evaluate the cost and pricing structure of each property management system. Consider both upfront costs, such as setup fees or licensing fees, as well as ongoing monthly or annual subscription fees. Compare the pricing plans and features offered to ensure you are getting value for your investment.

- **Demos and Trials:** Before making a final decision, request demos or trials of the property management systems that you are considering. This will allow you to test the functionality, explore the user interface, and assess whether the system meets your specific needs.

- **Recommendations and References:** Reach out to other vacation rental property owners or industry professionals to get recommendations and references. Hearing about their experiences with different property management systems can provide valuable insights and help you make an informed decision.

By following these steps and conducting thorough research, you can select an effective property management system that aligns with your needs, enhances your operational efficiency, and maximizes the success of your short-term vacation rental property investments.

CREATING A BOOKING AND RESERVATION PROCESS

A well-designed booking and reservation process can help attract potential guests, streamline the booking experience, and ensure a positive first impression. To implement this, you need to:

Utilize an Online Booking Platform

Utilize online booking platforms specifically designed for short-term vacation rentals, such as Airbnb, VRBO, or Booking.com. These platforms provide user-friendly interfaces and secure payment systems that facilitate the booking process. By listing your property on these platforms, you can reach a wide audience of potential guests and benefit from their built-in booking systems.

Provide Clear and Detailed Property Listing Policies

In your listing, it is important to clearly outline any house rules, check-in and check-out procedures, and cancellation policies. Providing detailed information upfront helps set clear expectations for guests regarding various aspects of their stay, including check-in and check-out times, house rules, noise restrictions, pet policies, smoking policies, and any other specific guidelines or restrictions. By clearly communicating these expectations upfront, you minimize misunderstandings and ensure guests are aware of what is expected of them during their stay.

Having well-defined policies also ensures consistency in how you manage your short-term vacation rental property. This consistency fosters fairness and equality among all guests. By applying policies consistently, you create a level playing field for guests, avoid potential biases, and maintain a professional and transparent approach to managing your property.

Clear policies will help you ensure that your short-term vacation rental property remains in compliance with local laws, regulations, and licensing requirements. By having policies that align with legal obligations, you protect yourself and your guests from potential legal issues. For example, policies related to occupancy limits, safety guidelines, or tax collection can help you adhere to local regulations and maintain a lawful operation.

Policies play a vital role in managing risks associated with short-term vacation rentals. For instance, policies regarding security deposits, cancellation policies, or liability waivers can help protect you from potential financial losses or damages caused by guests. Having clear policies in place also demonstrates your commitment to maintaining a safe and secure environment for guests, which can mitigate risks and potential liability issues.

Well-defined policies contribute to a positive guest experience and overall guest satisfaction. By providing clear guidelines and expectations, guests can have confidence in their booking and understand what to expect during their stay. This clarity can enhance their experience, minimize potential disappointments, and ultimately lead to positive reviews, recommendations, and increased guest satisfaction.

Maintain a Real-Time Availability Calendar

A real-time calendar provides accurate and up-to-date information on the availability of your property, allowing potential guests to see which dates are open for booking. This eliminates the need for back-and-forth communication with potential guests regarding date availability. Instead, guests can check availability, select their desired dates, and proceed with the booking process without delays. This efficient booking process enhances the overall guest experience and reduces the likelihood of losing potential bookings due to slow response times.

By maintaining a real-time availability calendar, you can also avoid double bookings or errors that may arise from manually managing reservations across multiple platforms or channels. The calendar serves as a centralized source of truth that automatically updates as bookings are made, ensuring that you never accept conflicting reservations and minimizing the risk of errors or oversights from manual intervention.

A real-time availability calendar will also allow you to track and analyze your property's occupancy rates accurately. By having a clear overview of your property's availability, you can identify periods of high and low demand, strategically adjust rates, and optimize occupancy. This helps maximize your rental income by filling vacant periods and adjusting rates to reflect market demand.

Use Automated Pricing and Minimum Stay Requirements

Set automated pricing rules and minimum stay requirements based on factors such as seasonality, day of the week, or length of stay. This helps ensure consistent and fair pricing for your property and encourages longer bookings or bookings during low-demand periods. You can also optimize rental rates based on factors such as demand, seasonality, market trends, and competitor prices.

Whether it's adjusting rates for holidays, local festivals, or high-demand seasons, automated pricing tools can apply predetermined rules to ensure you capture the increased demand and optimize revenue during these periods. This eliminates the need for manual rate adjustments and ensures consistent and accurate pricing throughout the year.

Implement Instant Booking or Request Approval

Consider offering instant booking for guests who meet your predetermined criteria, such as a minimum number of positive reviews or verification requirements. Alternatively, you can opt for a request approval system, where potential guests submit a booking request that you manually approve or decline based on availability and suitability.

Provide Prompt and Clear Guest Communications

Prompt and clear communication with guests is essential to ensure a positive guest experience and address any concerns or inquiries efficiently. Utilizing various systems and tools can help you achieve effective communication. Here are a few key systems to consider:

- **Automated Messaging Platforms:** These platforms allow you to create pre-set templates for common messages such as booking confirmations, check-in instructions, and post-stay follow-ups. By automating these messages, you can ensure prompt delivery of essential information while saving time and effort.

- **Guest Communication Portals:** Using a centralized platform for guests to access important information and communicate with you, these portals can include details about the property, local recommendations, FAQs, and the ability for guests to submit inquiries or request assistance. A guest communication portal ensures that guests have access to information at their fingertips and can easily communicate with you when needed.

- **Online Booking Platforms:** Leverage the built-in messaging and communication features provided by online booking platforms such as Airbnb, VRBO, or Booking.com to promptly respond to inquiries, booking requests, and messages from guests to provide quick and reliable communication throughout the booking and stay process.

- **Instant Messaging Apps:** Utilize instant messaging apps such as WhatsApp, Messenger, or SMS to maintain real-time communication with guests, enabling you to address guest inquiries promptly and efficiently. Be responsive and available to answer any questions or concerns that guests may have, ensuring a smooth and positive experience.

- **24/7 Customer Support:** Consider providing 24/7 customer support to address guest inquiries or emergencies at any time by hiring a dedicated support team or partnering with a professional property management company that offers round-the-clock guest support. Prompt and reliable support demonstrates your commitment to guest satisfaction and helps build trust and loyalty.

Prompt and clear communication systems help you establish a positive and reliable relationship with your guests and ensure effective communication throughout the guest journey and enhance their overall experience.

SECURE PAYMENT PROCESSING

Secure payment processing is paramount when managing short-term vacation rental investments. It not only protects your financial interests but also ensures a smooth and trustworthy transaction process for both you and your guests.

Reputable and secure payment processors like Stripe, PayPal, or Square offer robust security measures and encryption protocols to protect sensitive financial information. By integrating these payment gateways into your booking system or online platforms, you can ensure that guests' credit card details are handled securely and reduce the risk of data breaches or fraudulent activities.

Also, if you list your property on online booking platforms, take advantage of their secure payment processing features. These platforms often have built-in payment systems that handle transactions securely, protecting both you and the guest. Utilizing trusted and established booking platforms adds an additional layer of security to the payment process, as these platforms invest in robust security measures to protect guests' financial information.

Always clearly communicate your payment policies to guests upfront. This includes specifying payment methods accepted, outlining deposit requirements, cancellation policies, and any additional fees or charges. Transparent policies build trust with guests and ensure they are aware of the payment process and associated terms and conditions.

By implementing secure payment processing practices, you protect both your guests' financial information and your own financial interests. This fosters guest confidence, enhances your reputation as a trusted vacation rental manager, and ensures a smooth and secure transaction experience for everyone involved.

CONFIRMATION AND WELCOME MATERIALS

Once a booking is confirmed, promptly send a confirmation email or message to the guest with all relevant details such as reservation dates, check-in instructions, contact information, and any additional instructions or guidelines. Providing a warm welcome and ensuring guests have the necessary information before their arrival contributes to a positive guest experience.

Immediately after a booking is confirmed, it is important to send a personalized confirmation email or message to the guest. This communication should include essential details such as the reservation dates, the property address, and any specific terms or conditions related to their booking. Reiterate the payment details and provide clear instructions on how to proceed with the payment, if applicable. This confirmation reassures guests that their booking is confirmed and sets the foundation for a positive guest experience.

Prior to guests' arrival, it is also important to provide them with detailed arrival instructions to help guests feel welcomed and prepared for their stay. This should include clear directions to the property, check-in procedures, and any access codes or keys required. Explain parking arrangements, if applicable, and provide contact information for any on-site property managers or key holders. Consider including a visual map or diagram to help guests navigate to the property easily.

Also, include a comprehensive welcome packet or digital compendium that provides detailed information about the property and its amenities. Include instructions on how to use appliances, HVAC systems, entertainment systems, and any other important features. Outline house rules, such as smoking or pet policies, noise restrictions, and garbage disposal guidelines. Clearly communicate your expectations for guests' behavior and respect for the property. Providing this information upfront helps prevent misunderstandings and ensures that guests are aware of how to care for and enjoy the property responsibly.

Providing local recommendations is always a nice feature to enhance guests' experience. You can include a curated list of nearby attractions, restaurants, shopping areas, and recreational activities, as well as insider tips and suggestions based on your local knowledge, like hidden gems or popular events happening during their stay. This not only helps guests make the most of their visit, but also adds a personal touch that enhances their overall experience.

Also, ensure that guests have access to your contact information and a reliable point of contact in case any questions or issues arise during their stay. Include your phone number, email address, and any emergency contact numbers, and provide clear instructions on how to reach out for assistance, whether it's for maintenance issues, property-related questions, or any other concerns.

By providing comprehensive confirmation and welcome materials, you set the stage for a seamless and enjoyable guest experience. Clear and detailed instructions, property information, house rules, local recommendations, and accessible support contribute to guests feeling welcome, informed, and well-prepared for their stay. And this level of attention to detail fosters guest satisfaction, positive reviews, and increases the likelihood of repeat bookings and referrals.

AUTOMATED REMINDERS AND FOLLOW-UPS

Automated communication systems help ensure a smooth and positive guest experience by providing timely information, reminders, and follow-ups throughout the guest journey. It is a good practice to send automated pre-arrival reminders to guests a few days before their scheduled check-in date with essential details such as check-in instructions, access codes, parking information, and any special instructions or requirements. By sending pre-arrival reminders, you help guests feel prepared and informed, reducing the chances of confusion or last-minute inquiries.

If you have a payment schedule in place, automated payment reminders can help ensure that guests are aware of upcoming payment due dates. These reminders can be sent a few days or weeks in advance, depending on your payment terms. By automating payment reminders, you minimize the risk of missed payments and can promptly address any payment-related issues that may arise.

An automated check-out reminder will provide clear instructions to guests on departure procedures. These reminders can include reminders to return keys, instructions on how to handle garbage disposal, and any other specific requirements you have for check-out. By automating check-out reminders, you help guests complete their stay smoothly and ensure a smooth transition for the next guest.

After guests check out, an automated follow-up email or message can be sent to the guests to request feedback and reviews. These automated feedback requests can include a brief survey or a link to a review platform where guests can share their experience. Collecting guest feedback helps you understand their satisfaction level, identify areas for improvement, and gather testimonials that can be used to enhance your property's reputation.

Automated reminders and follow-ups save time, ensure consistent communication, and enhance the guest experience throughout their stay. By implementing a well-designed booking and reservation process, you can streamline the guest experience, minimize the potential for errors or miscommunications, and create a positive first impression for your short-term vacation rental property. This will contribute to guest satisfaction, encourage positive reviews, and increase the likelihood of repeat bookings.

HOW TO HANDLE GUEST REVIEWS

Managing guest reviews for your short-term vacation property is a crucial part of maintaining a successful rental business. These reviews not only provide feedback for improvement, but also play a significant role in attracting new guests.

The first step is actively encouraging your guests to leave a review after their stay. This can be done by sending a follow-up email or message thanking them for choosing your property and asking them to share their experience. Make this process as easy as possible, providing clear instructions and possibly even a link where they can leave their review.

When reviews start to come in, it's important to respond promptly and professionally, whether the review is positive or negative. For positive reviews, express your gratitude for their kind words and that you're delighted they enjoyed their stay. This not only shows appreciation to the guest but also demonstrates to prospective guests your active involvement and care for your guests' experiences.

Handling negative reviews can be a bit trickier but is equally, if not more, important. It's crucial to address any issues raised honestly and politely, demonstrating your commitment to providing excellent service. Always apologize for any shortcomings, regardless of the circumstances, and describe any actions you plan to take to prevent similar issues in the future. This shows prospective guests that you take feedback seriously and are dedicated to continuous improvement.

Another key aspect of handling guest reviews is learning from them. Reviews provide invaluable insights into what guests liked and didn't like about their stay. This feedback can guide you in making improvements, whether it's upgrading your amenities, making your check-in process more straightforward, or investing in professional cleaning services.

Managing a short-term vacation property is a multifaceted endeavor that requires careful attention to various aspects, including hiring the right property manager, handling guest reviews, and ensuring your property meets guests' expectations consistently. To maintain a successful vacation rental, it's crucial to provide a seamless booking experience, ensure the property is well-maintained and clean, and offer excellent customer service. With meticulous management and a commitment to continuous improvement, your short-term vacation property can be a profitable and rewarding investment.

CHAPTER 12

MAINTAINING AND UPGRADING YOUR VACATION HOME

A vacation home is no different than other homes in that it will require a degree of ongoing maintenance, as well as the occasional upgrade to continue to maintain and increase the overall value of your investment.

Inevitably, things will go wrong, and you need to have the ability to move quickly to make the repairs or adjustments necessary to make sure your tenants are not impacted.

When it comes to upgrades, there are things that will be financially feasible and get you a return on your upgrade investment, and then things that are adequate but may not provide a positive return on the cost of the upgrade.

It is important to have a good understanding of what the market wants and will pay a premium for, and what the market is not willing to pay for.

MAINTAINING YOUR VACATION HOME

Maintaining your short-term vacation rental property is crucial to ensure its longevity as a viable investment as well as to ensure positive guest experiences and reviews.

Regular cleaning is of utmost importance. Have you ever rented a vacation home and found that it did not meet up to your cleaning standards? Every guest expects to arrive at a clean, fresh-smelling property. This involves thorough cleaning after each guest's departure, including washing linens, sanitizing surfaces, and restocking essential supplies like toilet paper and soap.

Regular deep cleaning should also be part of the routine to maintain the property's appeal over time. This can include carpet cleaning, washing windows, and maintaining outdoor spaces. Get a cleaning crew in place that you trust and know will do an excellent job in maintaining the cleaning standards that your renters (and you) insist on having.

As I mentioned earlier, there will be times when things will stop working, which can create a reactive maintenance nightmare. However, regular inspections can help avoid larger issues down the line. This might involve regular checks of the heating and cooling systems, plumbing, electrical systems, and appliances.

Regular checks for any signs of wear and tear or potential safety issues are also crucial. Any necessary repairs should be addressed immediately to avoid escalating issues that could lead to costly repairs and potential negative guest experiences. If you want to minimize the repair nightmares that can happen at your vacation property, take the time to be proactive and do regular inspections.

You should also implement a preventative maintenance plan to address routine tasks and inspections. This may include servicing HVAC systems, cleaning gutters, checking roof condition, inspecting and maintaining appliances, and regularly changing filters. Preventative maintenance helps avoid major issues and prolongs the lifespan of your property's components.

Having a good grounds crew is essential to making sure that property looks beautiful when the renters pull up to the home. Maintain the landscaping, trim bushes, mow the lawn, and address any pest or weed control needs. Regularly check outdoor furniture, grills, and amenities to ensure they are clean and in good working condition.

Safety and security should be a priority to protect both your renters and your investment. Take the time to implement security measures to protect your vacation home. Install quality locks, consider an alarm system, and provide clear instructions to guests regarding security practices. Regularly check windows, doors, and entry points for any vulnerabilities.

One thing that is often overlooked by vacation homeowners is pest control. Different climates produce different pest issues. Make sure you regularly inspect your vacation home for pests, and implement preventative measures to control pests effectively. Seal any gaps or cracks, remove food sources, and consider professional pest control services to maintain a pest-free environment. You can also hire a pest control company to regularly treat your home to keep away those unwanted critters.

As you begin to set your roots in a community, build relationships with trustworthy and reliable service providers, including cleaners, maintenance professionals, contractors, and handymen. Select reputable professionals who are responsive, efficient, and have experience in vacation rental property maintenance. Having boots on the ground to swiftly address any issues that may arise is priceless, and having the ability to respond to issues quickly will often depend on how good and reliable your service providers are.

Although there will be times that things do go wrong, it is important to be responsive to issues reported by guests. Despite your best preventative efforts, problems may arise during a guest's stay. Having a system in place for guests to report issues and a reliable team, whether it's you or a property manager, that can respond quickly and effectively will help maintain guest satisfaction.

UPGRADING YOUR VACATION HOME

Trends and guest expectations can change over time. Periodic updates, whether upgrading the kitchen, adding smart home features, or simply changing the decor, can help keep your property attractive and competitive. Remember, your vacation rental is more than just a place to stay; it is an integral part of your guests' travel experience. Investing in upgrades for your short-term vacation rental can significantly enhance its appeal, increase occupancy rates, and justify higher rental fees.

The kitchen is one of the key areas guests look at when booking a vacation rental. Upgrading appliances to modern, energy-efficient models can be a selling point for many guests. Also, providing high-quality cooking utensils, pots, pans, and a well-stocked pantry with basic spices and condiments can make the kitchen more appealing for guests who prefer to cook during their stay. People choose vacation homes over hotels because they are looking to have some of the same conveniences as home, and the kitchen is a focal point for most homes. This is an area that almost always provides good returns to the money you spend.

Upgrading the bathroom also can significantly improve your property's appeal. Modern, clean, and well-functioning bathrooms are a must for any vacation rental. Consider updating old fixtures, improving lighting, or even adding luxury touches like a rain shower head or heated floors. Providing high-quality toiletries can also add a touch of luxury to the guest experience. People are willing to pay extra for a luxurious experience, and the bathroom is a good place to invest in.

Additionally, investing in comfortable, high-quality furniture, particularly beds, can make a substantial difference in guests' comfort and overall experience. A good night's sleep can highly influence a guest's review of your property. Providing high-quality linens, an assortment of pillow types, and possibly even a choice of mattress firmness can further enhance the guest's sleep experience.

There is nothing worse than going on a vacation to rest and recover, only to find an uncomfortable bed and pillow that keeps you from a good night's sleep. If you want bad reviews, use subpar bedding. Or pamper your renters with the rest and rejuvenation they came there for, and your reviews will reflect that top-shelf experience.

The living area is another important space to consider for upgrades. Investing in a large, high-definition smart TV, comfortable seating, and perhaps gaming consoles or a collection of board games can transform your living area into an entertainment hub. This can be particularly appealing for families or groups traveling together. Give people a magical place they can spend their time together enjoying one another's company, and you will be providing them with both an experience and memories.

Adding smart home features can also be a great upgrade. This could include keyless entry systems, smart thermostats for easy climate control, and smart speakers for music streaming. These can add a layer of convenience and modernity to your property that tech-savvy guests will appreciate.

Strong and reliable internet connectivity is essential for most vacation home guests. Upgrade the Wi-Fi infrastructure to provide high-speed internet access throughout the property. Ensure good coverage in all rooms, including outdoor areas, and consider offering additional amenities like streaming services or smart TVs. There are so many people who work remotely these days, and a strong internet connection is always a good investment.

Enhancing safety and security measures can add value to a vacation home. Install a security system, smoke detectors, carbon monoxide detectors, and fire extinguishers. Consider adding secure locks, outdoor lighting, and safety features like window locks or security cameras. It is also a good practice to add room safes to provide an extra layer of protection for tenants when they leave the home. People like to feel safe when they are at a vacation home, and good security provides one less thing for them to have to think about while they are enjoying their vacation.

If feasible, consider adding additional bedrooms or sleeping areas to accommodate more guests. Adding a bedroom might not make financial sense, but you can look for ways to expand the number of people the home can accommodate. There should be limits to your capacity, because putting too many people in a home can lead to additional wear and tear, but expanding the property's capacity can increase rental income potential and attract larger groups or families looking for vacation accommodations.

Lastly, consider enhancing the outdoor space if your property has it. Nearly everyone loves spending time outside during their vacation. Many spend their waking hours working in offices and jobs that do not get them outside. Adding comfortable outdoor furniture, a BBQ grill, or even a hot tub can increase the appeal of your property.

In warmer climates, a swimming pool might be the expectation for potential renters. With our properties in Costa Rica, we would not even consider a property that does not have a swimming pool. Without a pool, potential tenants would immediately eliminate us from consideration.

Also, improving the curb appeal of your vacation home helps to create a positive first impression. This can include landscaping enhancements, exterior painting, upgrading the entryway, adding outdoor lighting, and ensuring proper maintenance of the property's exterior.

When considering upgrades for your short-term vacation rental, think about the areas that will most significantly enhance your guest's comfort and convenienceProperly planned and executed property improvements can contribute to a higher occupancy rate and potentially higher rental fees. Invest in the spaces where people want to spend their time with one another.

CHAPTER 13

LONG-TERM INVESTMENT STRATEGIES

When investing in short-term vacation rentals, it is always a good idea to start with the end in mind. My long-term investment strategy revolved around my love for real estate investment and my love for travel. Because of these two things, I started a private equity fund that allowed me to do both. I was able to take my real estate brokerage, investment, and valuation background and create a business around my skills that gives me an opportunity to begin traveling the world looking at and purchasing investment opportunities.

Your mission and purpose for investing will likely be different than mine, but to find the most success in purchasing vacation homes it is essential to get a clear understanding of what your long-term goals are. This will provide you with a roadmap for what your investment journey will look like over your investment holding period.

EVALUATING EXIT STRATEGIES

When buying a vacation home, your exit strategy typically tends to be something that most people do not think about. However, an exit strategy is an important part of any real estate investment. It's the plan you implement when you're ready to sell or move on from your property. There are several ways to evaluate which strategy is right for you.

One option for an exit strategy is simply selling the property. This is often the first strategy that comes to mind, and it's straightforward—once you're ready, you list the property on the market. The main factor to consider here is timing. You want to sell when the market is in your favor to maximize the return on your investment. You'll need to consider market trends, property values in your area, and the overall condition of your property.

If your vacation rental is one of many properties in your portfolio, another exit strategy could be a 1031 exchange. This strategy allows you to sell your property and reinvest the proceeds in a new property while deferring capital gains tax. This is an attractive strategy if you're looking to upgrade to a more profitable property or if you're shifting your investment focus to a different area. However, the process has specific timeframes and rules to follow in order to avoid paying taxes, so careful planning and potentially professional advice are necessary.

You could also consider seller financing, where you sell the property but continue to act as the lender for the buyer. This can open up a larger pool of potential buyers and provide you with a consistent income stream. However, there's a risk that the buyer may default on their payments.

If your property has significant equity, you might also consider a cash-out refinance. This allows you to refinance your mortgage for more than you owe and pocket the difference, providing you with cash to invest elsewhere, while still retaining ownership of the property.

Evaluating an exit strategy for a vacation home investment involves considering various factors to determine the most suitable approach for your specific investment goals. Here are some key considerations:

Investment Objectives

Assess your investment objectives and determine the role the vacation home plays in achieving them. Are you looking for long-term appreciation, generating rental income, or a combination of both? Understanding your investment goals will help shape your exit strategy.

For our private equity fund, we have a projected hold period of seven to ten years because we want to provide annual distributions to our shareholders and also get appreciation over the hold period. A range of seven to ten years gives us the flexibility to sell the property when we feel it is at the upper-end of the market, and thus get the best appreciation rate possible.

Market Analysis

Evaluate the current and projected market conditions for vacation homes in the area where your property is located. Consider factors such as property values, rental demand, occupancy rates, and local regulations that may impact the market. Understanding market trends can help you make informed decisions about the timing of your exit strategy. There is nothing more powerful than knowledge, and by getting a deep understanding of the markets that you are considering, you will increase your chances for success.

Rental Performance

Review the historical rental performance of your vacation home investment. Assess the occupancy rates, rental rates, and overall profitability of the property. Consider the potential for future rental income and how it aligns with your investment goals. Evaluate whether the property has been consistently profitable or if changes in market conditions may impact its future performance. Look for properties in markets that have good historical rental rate growth or look for markets with significant upside.

In the Costa Rica markets we are considering, we have the choice to either go into a market that has seen significant appreciation and rental rate growth, or we can choose markets we feel are about to experience that exponential growth. Either one could provide the investment returns we are looking for, so we tend to diversify our investments in both types of markets.

Cash Flow Analysis

Conduct a cash flow analysis to understand the financial viability of your investment. Evaluate the income generated from rental operations, taking into account expenses such as property management fees, maintenance costs, insurance, taxes, and financing expenses. Assess the impact of these expenses on your net cash flow and how it aligns with your investment objectives.

Become a sophisticated investor who understands the fundamentals of cash flow, and you will have better control of your investments. This will also allow you the opportunity to have strong historical operating information (which is extremely valuable to investors) once you go to sell your home.

Financing Considerations

When assessing the financing arrangement for your vacation home investment, consider any outstanding mortgage, loan terms, and potential costs associated with selling or refinancing the property. Evaluate the impact of these factors on your overall return on investment and cash flow.

Make sure you are looking at your loan and how it relates to your long-term goals. As an example, with our fund, we only have a seven to ten-year holding period. Because of this, it would not make sense for us to take out a fifteen or thirty-year loan that had a prepayment penalty.

Tax Implications

Again, there are many investors or potential investors that are so caught up in the now, that they forget to consider what their investment looks like when they get to the end of their holding period and go to market to sell. Selling the property, converting it into a long-term rental, or exchanging it through a 1031 exchange can have varying tax consequences. So consult with a tax professional to understand the tax implications associated with different exit strategies before deciding on an exit strategy.

Market Demand and Trends

Evaluate the current and projected market demand for vacation homes in the area. Consider factors such as demographics, tourism trends, and the attractiveness of the location for vacation rentals. Assess whether the market conditions support the potential for future appreciation or if other factors may impact the property's value.

Taking a historical look at the demand factors will often give you a good snapshot of what the future will hold in the markets that you are considering. By understanding the demand in the area, you will have a better understanding of what your sale opportunities look like when you are ready for your exit strategy.

Risk Assessment

Conduct a thorough assessment to evaluate the potential risks associated with each exit strategy. Consider factors such as market volatility, regulatory changes, economic conditions, and the potential for unforeseen expenses or challenges.

Everyone has different levels of risk tolerance, so make sure your long-term investment decisions meet your needs and standards. Assessing the risks helps you make an informed decision and mitigate potential drawbacks.

Portfolio Diversification

Consider your overall investment portfolio and the role the vacation home investment plays within it. Evaluate whether diversifying your investments by reallocating capital to other asset classes may better align with your investment objectives and risk tolerance.

Or maybe one investment property is enough for you. That is good, too. When it comes to diversification, it is all about your goals and carving out the future you want on this very personal journey. We will go into greater detail about portfolio diversification later in this chapter.

Timing Considerations

Assess the timing of your exit strategy in relation to the real estate market and your investment goals. Evaluate whether current market conditions are favorable for selling or if it may be beneficial to hold the property for a longer period to maximize potential returns. Also, make sure you give yourself the flexibility and ability to sell the property when the markets are in the upper range of the cycles. The people who lose money in real estate tend to be the ones that have to sell, rather than the ones who have positioned themselves to be able to take advantage of an up real estate market.

Exit Strategy Execution

Once you have evaluated and selected an exit strategy, develop an execution plan. Determine the necessary steps, such as property preparation, marketing, and engaging professionals for a smooth transaction, and ensure that you have a clear timeline and contingency plans in place.

Evaluating an exit strategy for a vacation home investment requires careful analysis of your investment goals, market conditions, rental performance, financing arrangements, and overall feasibility of continuing as an investor.

POTENTIAL RESALE VALUE

Estimating the potential resale value of a short-term vacation rental means considering several factors. The resale value, also known as the after-repair value (ARV), is the price that a property is likely to sell for once it has been fully renovated and is in market-ready condition.

One of the first things you should do is look at the comparable sales, often called "comps," which are recent sales of similar properties in the same local area. When looking at comps, consider properties that share similar attributes with yours, such as size, age, number of bedrooms and bathrooms, and location. Understanding what other similar properties in the area have sold for is one of the best indicators of what you can potentially sell your home for. You can usually find this information online or with the help of a local real estate agent or real estate appraiser.

You also need to consider the condition of your property and any renovations or improvements you've made. If you've recently upgraded the kitchen or bathrooms, installed new appliances, or made other significant improvements, these can increase your property's resale value. However, any outstanding repairs or maintenance issues can decrease the value.

There are also improvement items that might not add value to your property. These are adequate repair items the market does not recognize as additional value or items that buyers would not be willing to pay additional money for. Make sure you are selective in the renovations or improvements you are making to your investment, and make sure they will pay!

The property's location and the local real estate market will also have a significant impact on resale value. For instance, if your vacation rental is in a popular tourist area with high demand for accommodations, it's likely to have a higher resale value. Additionally, broader market conditions can affect the resale value. If the local real estate market is doing well and property values are increasing, your property's resale value is likely to be higher. Again, your location attributes can be quantified by looking at other properties in your area that would be considered similar in location to your property.

The property's performance as a vacation rental can also impact its resale value. If your rental has a strong occupancy rate, great reviews, and solid income history, the property will be more attractive to potential buyers, especially those looking to continue operating it as a vacation rental.

This is why it is extremely important to operate your vacation home like a business and have strong financials to show to a potential purchaser. But good historical financials demonstrate that the property has been well managed, and it is easy to do an analysis of this type of investment. Stronger operating information with sophisticated investors behind a deal will typically lead to a stronger sales price.

It is also good to get a better understanding of future developments or changes in the area that can influence the property's resale value. For instance, if there's a new attraction opening nearby or significant infrastructure improvements planned, these could increase your property's value.

In Colorado, we tend to have a lot of ski areas, and it is important to get a good understanding of ski area expansion plans. Many times, when a new owner comes into a ski resort, they have major plans to expand the facilities. This leads to increased tourism and demand, which also tends to lead toward higher nightly rental rates and higher property values. Having a good grasp on what a community's future looks like will provide insights into what could potentially happen to your rental rates and property values.

CONVERTING YOUR VACATION HOME INTO A RETIREMENT PROPERTY

Converting your short-term vacation rental into a retirement home can be an exciting transition, but it is one that requires thoughtful planning and consideration. You'll need to shift your mindset from considering the property as an income generator to treating it as a permanent personal space.

One of the first things you need to do when looking at a property for this type of investment is to assess the property's suitability for your retirement lifestyle. Think about the location and its proximity to healthcare facilities, shopping, entertainment, family, and friends. Will you enjoy living there full-time, or does the location only appeal for short vacation periods? Is it a suitable place for aging with access to necessary services and support?

You also need to evaluate the home's layout and design from the perspective of aging in place. As you grow older, your physical abilities might change, so consider whether the house will continue to be comfortable and safe. Is it a single-story property, or does it at least have a bedroom and full bathroom on the ground floor? Are doorways and hallways wide enough to accommodate mobility aids if needed in the future? It is difficult to think about these things when you are younger, but time does go by quickly and our living needs are always changing.

Take into consideration the financial implications of this decision. If you've been depending on the rental income from the property, how will your finances be affected when that income stops? Be sure to factor in the ongoing costs of maintaining the home, property taxes, and potential homeowner's association feesThis should not be a deal breaker for you, but you need to have a firm grasp on how this transition will impact your financial planning.

To make things easier, develop a transition plan that outlines the necessary steps and timeline for moving from your current residence to the vacation home. Consider logistics such as selling or renting out your current home, coordinating the transfer of utilities, and handling address changes for official documents and services. These might seem like small things, but having a good plan in place will help you move through the transition quickly and efficiently.

It is also important to consider the tax implications of this move. Depending on how long you've owned and rented out the property and how much its value has appreciated, you could face a significant capital gains tax bill when you sell the property. However, converting it into your primary residence for a certain period before selling could reduce this tax. Make sure you have a good understanding of the tax structures that would have an impact on this type of exit strategy.

One of the last things you should consider is how you'll transition the space from a rental property to your personal home. This might involve redecorating to suit your tastes, replacing rental-grade furniture with pieces you love, and adding personal touches to make the house feel like home. You will have spent years owning this property and renting it to others, and now want to make it wholly yours.

Getting to the age of retirement and having an opportunity to live in a location that you absolutely love is an exciting option. With careful planning and professional advice, you can make this transition smoothly and start enjoying your retirement.

1031 EXCHANGES

A 1031 exchange, also known as a like-kind exchange, is a strategy that real estate investors use to defer capital gains taxes when selling a property. Named after Section 1031 of the U.S. Internal Revenue Code, it allows an investor to reinvest the proceeds from a sale into a new property of equal or greater value and use, hence "like-kind." This strategy can be particularly useful when selling a short-term vacation rental, as it allows you to reinvest in another property and continue generating rental income while deferring capital gains tax.

The first thing you should take note of is the strict timeline of a 1031 exchange. From the day you sell your vacation rental property, you have forty-five days to identify potential replacement properties and one hundred eighty days to close on the new property. These deadlines are firm and missing them can disqualify the entire transaction.

Another important aspect of a 1031 exchange is the "like-kind" requirement. This generally means that the property you sell and the property you buy must be of the same nature or character, even if they differ in quality or grade. In practice, this means you can exchange almost any type of real estate for another, as long as it's held for productive use in a trade or business or for investment. So, your short-term vacation rental could be exchanged for a residential rental property, a commercial property, or even raw land.

One crucial point to note is that the property must be held for investment or business purposes, not for personal use. The IRS has established that if you rent the property for at least fourteen days per year and limit personal use to less than fourteen days per year or 10% of the total days rented, it qualifies as investment property and is eligible for a 1031 exchange.

Remember that the new property must be of equal or greater value, and you must reinvest all the proceeds from the sale into the new property to completely avoid capital gains taxes. If the new property is of lesser value, or if you don't reinvest all the proceeds, you may still owe some capital gains tax.

A 1031 exchange can be a complex process and should be conducted with the help of a qualified intermediary who is experienced in these types of transactions. They hold the sale proceeds on your behalf until they are used to purchase the new property, ensuring you don't take constructive receipt of the funds, which could disqualify the exchange.

TAX-DEFERRED REAL ESTATE INVESTMENTS

Apart from 1031 exchanges, vacation homes may also offer potential tax benefits through the following avenues:

Rental Income

If you rent out your vacation home, you can take advantage of various tax deductions related to rental activities. This includes deductions for mortgage interest, property taxes, insurance, maintenance expenses, and depreciation. Consult with a tax professional to understand the specific deductions and limitations based on your individual circumstances.

Capital Gains Exclusion

If you use your vacation home as a primary residence for a certain period, you may qualify for the capital gains exclusion upon its sale. As of 2021, individuals can exclude up to $250,000 of capital gains from the sale of their primary residence ($500,000 for married couples filing jointly) if they meet specific ownership and use requirements. However, note that this exclusion does not apply to investment properties.

Vacation Rental Tax Rules

Different tax rules apply based on the length of time you personally use the vacation home versus renting it out. If you use the property for more than 14 days or 10% of the total rental days (whichever is greater), it is considered a "personal use" property. In such cases, deductions are limited to the portion of expenses that corresponds to the rental activity. Consult with a tax advisor to understand the specific tax rules for vacation rentals.

Depreciation Deduction

If you use your vacation home as a rental property, you may be eligible to claim depreciation deductions. Depreciation allows you to deduct a portion of the property's value over time as it experiences wear and tear. However, it's important to note that depreciation recapture taxes may apply when you sell the property.

Tax laws are complex and subject to change, so professional advice can help you maximize the tax benefits available to you while staying in compliance with all relevant regulations.

DIVERSIFYING YOUR REAL ESTATE PORTFOLIO

We briefly spoke about diversifying your portfolio earlier in this chapter, but this can be an important part of your investment journey, so I would like to expand on this strategy. Diversifying your vacation home real estate portfolio is a smart approach to mitigate risk, capitalize on different markets, and maximize potential returns.

Here are some ways to diversify your vacation home holdings.

Geographic Locations

Invest in vacation homes located in different geographic areas like various regions, cities, or even different countries. By spreading your investments across different locations, you reduce the risk of being heavily impacted by local market fluctuations or regional economic conditions.

My private equity fund does not have all of our eggs in just one basket. We work relentlessly to find high-potential markets to invest in, but we do not invest in a single market. By investing in multiple markets, we reduce the risk of a single market underperforming and keeping us from reaching our investment goals and expectations. Being in multiple markets allows us to move out of the underperforming markets and double down in the highest-producing markets.

Vacation Destinations

Explore diverse vacation destinations with different appeals and attractions. This can include beachfront properties, mountain retreats, lake houses, urban getaways, or properties near popular tourist destinations. Diversifying your vacation home locations allows you to cater to different traveler preferences and target diverse rental markets. It also gives you an opportunity to go to different locations with varying amenities.

If you buy that house by the beach, you might find yourself spending all your time at the beach. If you buy the house by the ski slopes, you may feel stuck with just heading up into the mountains. But having different options with different amenities gives you choices and variety, which, as you know, is the spice of life!

Property Types

In addition to location, you can also diversify your vacation home portfolio by investing in different types of properties like condominiums, villas, cabins, townhouses, or even unique properties like yurts or treehouses. Each property type attracts different types of travelers and offers unique rental income potential.

Rental Strategies

It is also a good idea to adopt different rental strategies for your vacation homes. Consider offering short-term rentals, long-term rentals, or a combination of both. Explore platforms like Airbnb, VRBO, or traditional rental channels to diversify your rental income streams.

The key here is to find what is working. As with anything, you should always be willing to test, optimize, and scale—meaning you should test different methods to see what is working best, optimize those efforts to get the best investment results, then scale those results to maximize your efforts and ultimately your returns.

Seasonal Demand

Invest in vacation homes with varying seasonal demand. Some locations may experience peak demand during specific seasons or holidays, while others may have more consistent year-round demand. By diversifying across properties with different seasonal patterns, you can optimize rental income throughout the year and have operating income continuously coming in based on the varying seasons. It also allows you an opportunity to focus on one property during its high season, and then rotate your focus to the other property when it is in its peak season.

PROPERTY SIZES

Diversify the sizes of vacation homes in your portfolio—smaller properties for couples or smaller families and larger properties to accommodate larger groups or multiple families. Offering a range of property sizes expands your target market and rental income potential.

Amenities and Features

Invest in vacation homes with different amenities and features. Some travelers may prefer properties with beach access, private pools, hot tubs, game rooms, or proximity to specific attractions. By diversifying the amenities and features of your properties, you can attract a broader range of guests and increase your booking potential.

Market Segments

Explore different market segments within the vacation rental industry. This can include targeting family-friendly vacation homes, luxury properties, pet-friendly accommodations, or properties suited for adventure and outdoor activities. Each market segment has its own characteristics and potential for rental demand.

Property Management

Utilize different property management strategies for your vacation homes. Consider self-managing some properties while outsourcing the management of others to professional vacation rental management companies. This provides diversification in terms of management style and expertise, and it also allows you the opportunity to test what works best for you. No property management system has to be forever, and if you try multiple options, you will eventually decide upon the best option for you and your investment strategy.

Exit Strategies

Plan for different exit strategies for each vacation home. This can include selling properties, converting them into long-term rentals, or transitioning them into personal-use residences. Having multiple exit strategies allows flexibility in responding to market conditions and changing personal circumstances.

CHAPTER 14

TAKING THE NEXT STEPS

know this is a lot of information to take in, but it is critical that you understand the valuation methodology and fundamentals that will help you reduce your risk as you go down this very exciting path.

I have spent years in the real estate business, and there is nothing quite like the thrill of securing a highly lucrative real estate investment property. Short-term vacation rentals have provided me not only with income opportunities, but the ability to build my life around two things I love—real estate investment and travel.

As you pursue short-term vacation rental investments, I encourage you to master the fundamentals provided throughout this book and put in the time and the due diligence to be exceptional as you progress on this journey.

TAKING ACTION

In the realm of investment possibilities, vacation homes provide incredible opportunity and potential. Now is the time to use the fundamentals in this book to break free from hesitation and embark on a journey that can bring both financial rewards and personal fulfillment.

Here are just a few reasons why you should take action and start investing in vacation homes.

A Path to Financial Freedom

Investing in vacation homes offers a pathway to financial freedom. By generating steady rental income, you can unlock a new stream of revenue that grows with each booking. Imagine the financial security and independence that can come from building a portfolio of vacation homes, where your investments work for you, even while you relax on a beach or explore the wonders of the world.

Diversification for Stability

Diversifying your investment portfolio is a wise strategy to safeguard against market volatility. Vacation homes provide an opportunity to expand beyond traditional investments, such as stocks or bonds. By spreading your assets across real estate, you create a solid foundation that can withstand the unpredictable tides of the financial market, offering stability and resilience in times of uncertainty.

The Joy of Ownership

Owning a vacation home is not just about financial gains; it's about embracing a lifestyle of joy, adventure, and cherished memories. Picture yourself stepping into your very own retreat, a place where you can escape the ordinary to experience the extraordinary. Your vacation home becomes a sanctuary, a haven where you can create lasting moments with loved ones, bask in the beauty of nature, and recharge your spirit.

Expanding Horizons

Investing in vacation homes opens doors to new horizons, both figuratively and literally. It allows you to explore diverse locations, immerse yourself in different cultures, and discover hidden gems around the world. From beachside havens to mountain retreats, there are endless possibilities to expand your investment footprint and create a portfolio that reflects your passions and dreams.

Growing Demand for Experiences

In an era where experiences reign supreme, vacation rentals are in high demand. Travelers seek unique, personalized accommodations that provide the comforts of home and the allure of adventure. By investing in vacation homes, you position yourself at the forefront of this thriving market, tapping into a growing pool of travelers who crave authentic and memorable experiences.

Unleashing Your Entrepreneurial Spirit

Investing in vacation homes allows you to unleash your entrepreneurial spirit. You become a visionary, a creator of opportunities, and a master of your own destiny. With each property you acquire, you have the chance to shape its identity, design its ambiance, and craft an unforgettable experience for guests. The power to create and innovate is in your hands.

Leaving a Legacy

By investing in vacation homes, you create a lasting legacy for yourself and future generations. Your properties become tangible symbols of your hard work, determination, and foresight. They are a testament to your achievements and provide a foundation for your loved ones to build upon. Through vacation home investments, you leave a lasting impact on the lives of those who follow in your footsteps.

So, take action now and unlock the doors to a world of opportunity. Embrace the journey of investing in vacation homes, where financial rewards, personal fulfillment, and cherished memories await. Step into the realm of possibility and let your investments flourish amidst the beauty of vacation destinations. The time is ripe, and the rewards are within reach. Start investing in vacation homes today, and watch your dreams transform into a vibrant reality.

I always enjoy learning about your personal journeys and experiences. Make sure you connect with me and let me know about both your trials and tribulations as you embark on this amazing journey.

Here are the places that you can connect with me:

RODMAN SCHLEY

- **LinkedIn** | linkedin.com/in/rodmanschley
- **YouTube** | youtube.com/@gorodman
- **Instagram** | instagram.com/gorodman
- **Facebook** | facebook.com/gorodman
- **TikTok** | tiktok.com/@gorodman

BLUE FUSION CAPITAL

- **LinkedIn** | linkedin.com/company/bluefusioncapital
- **YouTube** | youtube.com/@bluefusioncapital
- **Instagram** | instagram.com/bluefusioncapital
- **Facebook** | facebook.com/bluefusioncapital
- **TikTok** | tiktok.com/@bluefusioncapital

Additional sources for real estate terms defined in Chapter 4:

- **Real Estate Purchase Price:** *Real Estate Principles: A Value Approach* by David Ling and Wayne Archer, which provides a comprehensive introduction to the real estate industry.

- **Real Estate Closing Costs:** "Shopping for Your Home Loan: HUD's Settlement Cost Booklet" by the U.S. Department of Housing and Urban Development, the complete guide to closing costs.

- **Average Daily Rate (ADR):** "Hotel Management and Operations" by Michael J. O'Fallon and Denney G. Rutherford, which provides coverage of the hotel industry and its operations, including the use of performance metrics like ADR.

- **Occupancy Rate:** "The Vacation Rental Goldmine: How to Maximize Your Rental Income With Great Guest Experiences" by Chris DeBusk, which provides insights into managing and optimizing vacation rental properties.

- **Appreciation Rate:** "Real Estate Finance and Investments" by William B. Brueggeman and Jeffrey Fisher, which provides an overview of real estate investment concepts including property appreciation.

- **Potential Gross Rental Income:** "The Complete Guide to Real Estate Finance for Investment Properties" by Steve Berges, an overview of financial analysis techniques for real estate.

- **Adjusted Gross Rental Income:** *Investing in Real Estate* by Gary W. Eldred, a guide to real estate investment strategies and financial analysis techniques.

- **Net Operating Income:** *The Real Estate Investor's Guide to Cash Flow and Equity Management: Choose the Investing Strategy to Maximize Your Goals* by Jack Cummings. This book offers an in-depth look at real estate financial metrics.

- **Net Cash Flow:** *Real Estate Finance & Investments* by William Brueggeman and Jeffrey Fisher, a guide to understanding the risks and rewards of investing in residential and commercial real estate.

- **Capitalization Rate (Cap Rate):** *Real Estate Finance & Investments* by William Brueggeman and Jeffrey Fisher, a guide to understanding the risks and rewards of investing in residential and commercial real estate.

- **Average Annual Rate of Return:** "The Handbook of Real Estate Portfolio Management" by Joseph Gyourko, an overview of managing and investing in real estate.

www.ingramcontent.com/pod-product-compliance
Lightning Source LLC
Chambersburg PA
CBHW081809200326
41597CB00023B/4197